Communication from the
Awakening of Humanity — Volume Three

Thought Reality

Mark Allen Frost

Seth Returns Publishing

Copyright © 2008 by Mark Allen Frost
First Edition
Published by Seth Returns Publishing

Editorial:
Mark Frost with assistance from Carol Sterritt-Frost
Cover Art, Design, Typography & Layout: Mark Frost

Library of Congress Control Number: 2007903854
ISBN 10: 0-9740586-4-5
ISBN 13: 978-0-9740586-4-1
Printed in the U.S.A.

Dedicated to my wife Carol Joy, without whose help

I would probably not be alive to see this beautiful day,

and of course to Seth and his gracious readers.

CONTENTS

Dialogue: Improvements on Both Sides
Positive Realities
Findings
Lessons
Ego and Soul
Intellectualization
Denial
Mass Denial
advocate teacher speaker
Exercise: Consolidate Your Findings

Dialogue: Does Seth Feel Emotion?
Reality Creation
Unconscious Creation
Example - Unconscious Creation

CONTENTS

CONTENTS

CONTENTS

Helpful Info From Carol Sterritt-Frost

While you are pursuing your studies with Seth, please visit
our website sethreturns.com. There you will find a Glossary and other
tools to assist you on your journey.

Do not use any of the information in this book in place of any medical
advice or treatment.

INTRODUCTION BY MARK

Here we are once again with a new Seth book. Thank you for your interest in our project. I thought you would be interested in how we put these books together. The way it works is that Seth first tells me the general title of the book, the approximate number of pages and the titles of the chapters. Then I take Seth's dictation wherever and whenever I can. Seth will open up the session by saying, "This piece will go with the chapter on the Vanguard," or some other introductory statement. Then he will dictate the material. Sometimes a session will last only 10 minutes. Sometimes I have time for a 30 minute session. I enter a light Trance and channel his communication stream, taking down the information in writing or on my computer. When Seth tells me we have enough for a book, we begin the editing process. What we have to work with are "little essays," as Seth calls them. I enter a light Trance and let Seth do the editing. He very seldom alters any of the content of the dictation. Mainly Seth connects the pieces into wholes under the chapter headings.

You will find that the format is nearly identical to the first two books in the series. I kept the Dialogues for this final volume, as I thought that by revealing a bit of personal information to begin each chapter would demonstrate how I interact with my Guide - Seth. I am also noting when Seth expresses himself in a humorous way. I hope I am not over-doing it. Most readers can probably tell when he is being funny without my little notations, but I do want to confirm when Seth is being intentionally funny.

We capitalize terms such as Energy Personality for easier reading and because we have no indexing. We use a large font because it makes for easier reading. (I realize this is a debatable issue.) Seth suggested that I not include copious notes and that I include his made-up words like "imaginal" and "theoretical." He asked me to leave his sometimes un-usual wording and syntax alone.

I put in timestamps for the Dialogues and for the Q and A to give readers a timeline for this material. I thought it would be good for people to see how long it takes Seth to create an answer to a personal question, and so I include beginning and ending times in that section of the Q and A. .... denotes a short pause in Seth's dictation.

As I write this intro I have just read the book in its entirety and I am once again amazed at what he can accomplish. Seth has created a very potent book. It is a kaleidoscope of interesting ideas and experiments. Now that I am free to do some reading and experimenting, I am going to take his advice and start creating some positive realities. Won't you join me?

INTRODUCTION BY SETH

In our new material together we have created a dialogue. Mark has defined the term dialogue in an amusing
way, as a simple matter of attempting to stay out of the
way and allowing me "to talk through." Yet it is quite
literally true that if you are to establish and continue
communications with your Energy Personality and other
guides, you too will of necessity learn how to get out of
the way of your own thoughts, images and beliefs to allow
your Guides "to talk through" you.

The development of communications with the Higher
Self may evolve slowly over time. Some of my readers who
have contacted us have described the difficulty in making
that initial contact. This process is as difficult to understand
and participate in as your openness to these spiritual matters.
It is a matter of distracting the ego/intellect consistently over
time, so that cynical judgments of futility and hopelessness
are less likely to be made.

We have spoken before of the ego's delight in creating
diversions of its own, to divert the student's awareness from
demonstrations of the essentially metaphysical or spiritual
basis of physical reality. The ego/intellect feels that it will
be washed away, as in a flood of emotion, if this inner

world is acknowledged to any degree. Therefore, I urge you to create your moment-to-moment distractions, when you are receiving divine information while meditating, for example, or perhaps while simply walking in nature. Create your diversions and say to yourself, "Look at this. Here in the inner world is where the adventure begins." Eventually you will succeed in diverting the censor of the ego/intellect long enough to experience your little awakenings. You will meet your Energy Personality and your other Guides. The cynicism and hopelessness will fade away.

THE MAGICAL PERSPECTIVE

In this book I hope to assist you and others that you may bring on board here, in discovering the unknown reality of the Soul. Already many of you are making great strides in this endeavor. You are changing to a different perspective. This perspective I have referred to as the magical perspective in my early manuscripts. So this material is not new to the student of my collected works. Yet I am again EMPHA-SIZING these important concepts here in the new material, in the hope that the reader will quite seriously pursue the quest for the sacred lenses of perception, the Inner Senses. Now remember, the Inner Senses will allow you this vantage point, the magical perspective. These senses are quite simply the perceptive apparatus of the magician, the shaman, the witch and the healer.

I have mentioned that the magical perspective and thus the use of the Inner Senses was a great deal more common-place in your perceived past, than now in this current time-frame. You might say that EVERYONE had at least a touch of these perceptual powers and indeed they exercised these powers in their daily lives. There was a "group mind" effect operative in those eras, that created a sacred unity among the people of any given area. This sharing of cosmologies that was such a cohesive factor in the ancient peoples of your Earth is sorely lacking in your modern times.

If I may digress for a moment, I would assert that your television and other mass media have supplanted this group mind phenomenon with a system of coercion that tends to reinforce ideas and images that support commerce and the growth of industry, certainly at the expense of these ideas of shared culture and spirituality. Your allegiances to your brothers and sisters have given way to an unwavering support for corporations and the products they produce. Many of you now equate the giving of mass-produced items of various types with the giving of Love. This is merely one example of how you have distanced yourselves from "the things that really matter," in your terms.

Fortunately, this cohesiveness I am describing is not lost forever. Memories of the time spent in the Mystery Civilizations are welling up to the surface of awareness for great numbers of you. The Turnabout in thought and behavior is manifesting. And all of you, simply through your psychic alliance with the Seth Entity, are capable of achieving this state of consciousness. This is a curative measure here as consciousness seeks to correct imbalances in the creation of mass realities within a particular people. Evolutionary consciousness seeks to re-establish a sense of group cohesion, shared spiritual values and other attributes within the "tribe" for purposes of its own continued growth and Value Fulfillment. In a sense, you may think of my messages to you in Third-Dimensional Reality as representative of evolutionary consciousness - the great loving creative energy of All That Is. Good luck with your studies.

PREFACE

The centerpiece of this current work is our treatise on healing - The Healing Regimen. The other regimen, Spiritual Prosperity, is also important, in that it provides methods for the creation of positive realities. The chapter on Wisdom Lessons was created to teach the reader how to approach the creation of the positive from the negative in broad terms. It was thought that Mark and I would create protocols and procedures for the reader to follow and "embody" that would assist them in creating balance within the three domains we briefly covered in our last book - health, wealth and wisdom. Once the basic needs were met you could THEN take this information to the world. In other words, this material is offered to you so that you may awaken and assist in the awakening of others.

All of the remaining chapters are presented as supportive information. We are once again covering material we presented in my latest books. We are also offering you many ideas not yet presented in the new Seth manuscripts or the old Seth material for that matter. We are attempting to tie together the many strands of information that you require to further your evolution as a Soul. As always, our advice is to take what suits your needs. There should be something within these pages to assist each and every one of you, regardless of your state of development in the material or in the nonphysical worlds.

CHAPTER ONE

The Research Project

Dialogue - Improvements on Both Sides
8/31/06 10:02 AM

Mark: *Anything at all Seth?*
Seth: *Yes Mark, I am quite pleased with the progress we are making in our readings and questions. The last question was particularly valuable, I think, in that both yourself and the client were able to see where improvements could be made within your own individual personalities. Now for the work at hand. A moment...*

Positive Realities

Hello again Dear Reader. Welcome to the Research Project. Our subject for this volume is the creation of positive realities, an important skill that may be learned by the serious student of metaphysics. This new book is definitely within the genre of metaphysical literature, I am certain you will agree. We are presenting our ideas in the vernacular of the seeker within nonphysical reality, the human on a quest for self-understanding. I am a nonphysical being and so you might think of me as having a more direct relationship with the elements of nonphysical reality than do you. My perspective is one of direct experiencing of my own multidimensional existence, my many lives. Briefly, it is my mission to give you the benefit of my expansive perspective here, to assist you in broadening your own perspective.

For some of you this will not present much difficulty in studying and assimilating the ideas and theories in these pages. You relish the challenge of examining your behaviors and beliefs in detail, and then attempting to change them. For others the going may be more complicated and entail a greater focusing of the human energies to the task of self-exploration and belief change. Yet might I suggest that ALL of you, those of my readers who are more accepting and those who may be resisting these messages, are already successful? In the probable realities created by your consciousness, you are successful in your studies. Each positive thought that you entertain within your mental environment, each moment that you are successful in fending off cynicism, denial, fear and anxiety, serves as a foundational support within these probable realities. These premanifestation domains are literally "fueled" by your positive thoughts. Now there is a "tipping point," as Mark has described this term to me, as the enrichment of these potential realities creates a state of imminent manifestation. The Positive Consensus Reality is rapidly moving from the probable to the actual.

As we have discussed before, linear time is a useful fiction for you in Third-Dimensional Reality, and so when I speak of positive realities moving from imminent to actual, I am using your terminology and your useful theories of time and space. In actuality, from my perspective and indeed from your perspective as a Soul, there always exists the probability that you may experience the immediate transformation of your reality, as in spontaneous healings of various types, and as in the wholesale transformation of beliefs that may come with religious conversion. Indeed, it is just this perspective that I am attempting to cultivate within the Personal Reality of the reader. Let us begin.

Findings

In my last book I asked you to embody the role of Scientist of Consciousness. The laboratory for you was your own mental environment and your self-created reality, what we have named the Personal Reality Field. Your Reality Field is a reflection of your ongoing mentality, as you create Reality Constructs from the infinite probabilities available to you. Thus, the Research Project will be quite different for each of you. Your experiences will vary tremendously according to individual personality aspects and activities in the "real" world.

Now let us discuss what are to be the Findings that you will bring to this project. As I have stated in the introduction, it is a good idea for you to have read these new books of mine. Having said that I must ask you, "What have you learned about yourself?" "Have you discovered what are your primary and secondary Lessons for You-the-Soul?" "Are you experiencing progressive Soul Evolution currently, or are you stagnant, perhaps denying what you have come to Earthly existence to learn?" These are all necessary questions to be answered before we progress to the next level of understanding here in this collaboration. Therefore, it would be wise to take some time to answer these questions in writing. This will establish a benchmark that you may refer to as we proceed. Please see our exercise at the end of this chapter.

Lessons

This is an advanced book on the subject of Reality Creation. It is assumed that you have developed the skills of self-observation described in the new material, or perhaps you have read other Teachings on the subject of receiving and translating divine information. As an advanced work, we shall take it for granted that you are learning your Lessons. As you well know, the Lessons for you in physical reality are the emotional states of anger, fear, shame, racial prejudice and others, that you must transform with your Intent into Loving Understanding and Courage. In this way, our system is quite similar to others that you may have known in your life as a seeker of knowledge. This makes sense, does it not? The seeker of wisdom tries as many systems as necessary until they have realized the Soul's Intent.

Ego and Soul

I have suggested that your main task in physical reality is to participate willingly in this exercise, as though you were in a school, for you are indeed in an educational relationship with your Third-Dimensional Reality. You the reader are both teacher and student. Your greater personal consciousness, what we have been calling the Soul in these works, acts as a teacher to your Earthly ego. On the subtle levels, You-the-Soul know full well what are your Lessons for your current incarnation.

The ego, what we are calling the student aspect in this description, "pretends" to be unaware of these life Lessons and their dramatization in physical reality. This is "the play" of your physical world - your creation of learning experiences in ensemble with other humans, for your mutual edification, and for the greater experiencing of All That Is. I have covered this quite thoroughly in the new material, and so I shall not digress. However, please take from this brief reminder this fact of existence: just as many other teachers both physical and metaphysical have stated, "Each second of your Earthly experience is an opportunity for spiritual growth. The way to move forward in your Soul Evolution, is to perfect the transformation of Negative Emotions into their divine counterparts."

Now this quest for self-realization may be short if you are prepared to face your Lessons directly, without the denial and avoidance for which humans are so famous. To those of us in the higher dimensions, it can appear as quite strange how many of you continue to suffer the effects of anger, fear, and the like, all the while knowing full well how you may extricate yourselves from your dilemma. Here I am referring to the continuous messages from Beings of Light that exist within your mental environments, yet which you ignore through various mental and physical maneuvers. Perhaps I should take a moment here, before we get into the substance of the book, to describe for you these incredible gymnastics of consciousness. (humorously)

Intellectualization

One of the most popular forms of avoidance for you is intellectualization. Through this strategy you assess the divine information within your mental sphere as something completely explainable. Scientific reasoning - logical deduction - is used to place the information in a neat and tidy and already known and understood category. Here a stream of spiritually-informed communication is interrupted and redirected to other parts of the psyche where it will not cause any disruptions. To continue this metaphor, the stream of Divine Information attempts to erode or melt away the self-limiting beliefs within the psyche - beliefs that may no longer serve the purposes of the evolving Soul. But the ego is in charge here, and the strategy of intellectualization works quite well for the majority of you. It allows you to ignore, as mere mental anomalies, these messages from your Higher Self. A brief example: when you experience a viewing of a nonphysical being - a "spirit" in your terms - you ascribe the sensory information you are receiving to "tricks" of the eyes, being perhaps mentally exhausted, hallucinations due to any number of "rational" causes. I am certain that the reader may contribute their own examples.

Of course in the workplace this strategy allows you to keep focused on the task at hand. In your private lives the misdirection of the ego/intellect allows you to continue on your path of development, however nonproductive and even self-destructive this path might be. Indeed, it seems that the more nonproductive the life lived, the more firmly the ego intellectualizes - "explains away"- the information received from the Divine Source.

Denial

With denial you have another very successful strategy for avoiding your Lessons. Here you are literally creating a reality for yourself unconsciously, and then disavowing any hand in the creation of that reality. "I am innocent," you are in effect saying. Yet obviously it is your world that you are co-creating here. Your Personal Reality Field certainly bears the marks of your personality. Still, when you are up against something that you do not wish to face - perhaps because it is embarrassing to you, something quite true, yet something that challenges your standards - you disaffirm it, you disempower it, you DENY it. You deny the thing with vehemence relative to the importance you place upon it. In other words, you deny what you most know to be the utter truth, in the honest appraisal of the subject at hand.

Here again, those of us who observe your behavior, and know your motives and indeed your probable developmental paths as human beings, must laugh at such nonsense. The amount of energy wasted in such denials of self - for that is what these instances truly represent - is vast beyond all comprehension. And so we must laugh to ourselves, as we observe you in the midst of your "issues."

For example: when you experience a twinge of Negative Emotion, perhaps triggered by something in your environment that reminds you of an event, a negative event from your past, you immediately redirect the ego/intellect to something other than the negative memory, the negative event.

Now you may use this skill of distracting the ego/intellect to your advantage within Reality Creation programs described in this manuscript. The key to use of this technique is to FIRST listen to what the information stream is attempting to convey to you. Listen and understand. "Face the music," to coin a phrase.

In this sense, you have the opportunity for awakening to your denial in each and every one of your self-created moments. This current Moment Point, as you are reading this book, may become a moment of awakening if you but merely CONSIDER, that what you most ardently deny - particularly with regards to your so-called "issues" - may be better embraced as the truth of the matter. This is a simple test that you may utilize in assessing any perceived fact of life in your current existence. What do you most fear? What do you hate most strongly? Herein lie your weaknesses in your Reality Creation agendas. Inconsistencies, prejudices, cultural delusions, artifacts of consciousness that cause you to grimace or wince inwardly may be indicators of this denial of the Soul Self.

Mass Denial

Perhaps other examples are necessary to help pull you from your denial. (humorously) Many of you are most probably familiar with the denial of the drug addict or the alcoholic. In these instances it is very clear-cut. The subject may be experiencing the destruction of all that they hold most dear - family, business, friends, it is all falling away - yet still they maintain their "innocence." This is denial at its most obvious. But the negative effects of denial are also felt in every other sphere of human activity.

In the Consensus Reality Manifestation there is evidence of mass-created denial at work. Witness how the many millions of you in the West still deny your responsibility in the creation of negative conditions in the lives of those who live in developing nations. You are the squanderers of your Mother Earth's resources. You in the West use a great deal more of the oil, minerals, lumber etc. relative to population than do those in the poor developing countries. The rationalization here, a common one, is to state, perhaps under your breath, that "these people deserve their lot in life. They may be lazy. They merely have to pull themselves up by their own bootstraps," and so on. I have chastised you quite gently for these offenses in our last two books. I now continue this tradition in our final book in this series. (humorously)

Now I am aware that you are a student of mine and you are attempting to "work" on yourself. You are attempting to learn your Lessons and perhaps you are awakening from your denial. But please also notice the residual aspect of denial that is always with you in this regard. It is the seed from which racism and other unsavory misperceptions and misjudgments grow.

advocate teacher speaker

You are the project, Dear Reader. You are the one on the path of Soul Evolution. You are the one learning your Lessons in physical reality. And so this life you are living intensifies, in a way, when you have the intention of viewing it as a Sacred Quest. I do hope that you take my advice and address these matters with the seriousness they deserve.

Now, there will be humor for us to share in these voyages, to be sure. Your very lives are born in Love and Good Humor. And I have described to you in my second book the value of teaching moments of humor in your own lives. There are reincarnational dramas and there are also comedies, but first let us confirm the serious responsibility you take on when you begin and continue this research project of the Soul.

You are responsible. Whether you believe me or do not believe me when I suggest that you are a member of The Seth Entity, simply by virtue of the fact that you are reading this spiritual literature and perhaps actively participating in the exercises and experiments suggested, you are preparing yourself for the role of advocate, teacher, speaker. Think for a moment. Are you absorbing this material so that you may take advantage of your fellow humans? Most probably not. Just as the many readers of **Seth Speaks** and my other earlier works, pursued those studies for altruistic purposes, that is, for the pursuit of self-knowledge and a means to help others see the true picture of physical reality, so too are you engrossed in this Teaching for purposes of your own awakening, and most assuredly, so that you may spread the message to others.

You see, that is what you do. You are quite possibly of a type of personality that Loves this sort of literature. In many bodies, past, present and future, you are in all likelihood a student of these occult sciences. Perhaps now it is a good thing to admit to yourself if this is so. Now let us conduct some research into these ideas we have just discussed.

Exercise - Consolidate Your Findings

In a few brief sentences, can you articulate your orientation to physical reality and how you engage in this co-creation activity we have been discussing? Consider instances throughout your life when you were held back in your Soul's Evolution by the personality aspects exhibited in your Findings. Collect your Findings from past experimentation, either from my system or others with which you are familiar. If you have yet to conduct your experiments in this manner, take some time to make a list of the complaints and the positive observations that friends and family members, coworkers and others have registered about you in your life. Here we will take these assessments by your fellow humans as "true" at face value. At the end of this manuscript, you may decide that these assessments of you are not true. You are the final judge in these matters.

For example: are you known as self-centered, unwilling to help others, overly concerned about your appearance and the way you are perceived by others? Do people call you "egotistical?"

Have your friends referred to you as too gullible, perhaps easily taken advantage of, too willing to part with your money for unworthy causes?

Do your colleagues refer to you as the "salt of the Earth?" Do your friends admire you for your positive personality characteristics?

Who Are You?

Briefly document your Findings from your past experimentation. You may attempt this documentation in the manner of automatic writing, in a sense, taking dictation from your Energy Personality, as Mark does with me. Or you may simply put some words down, while you are in a light Trance referring to your notes. Do what seems best for you.

Document Your Findings Here

_____
_____
_____
_____
_____
_____
_____
_____
_____
_____
_____
_____
_____

CHAPTER TWO

Your Thought-Created World

Dialogue - Does Seth Feel Emotion?
4/30/05 2:10 PM

Mark: I have just read the preceding material. It is excellent, as usual.
Seth: Thank you Mark. And in answer to your telepathic inquiry, yes I am capable of "feeling" gratitude. Anger is not my strong suit, however. I believe I may beyond the hate, anger and fear that is stressed in your dimension.

Reality Creation

In this chapter we will present the basics for you. The phenomenon we are calling Reality Creation will be discussed in a very simplified form. Though we will certainly add to my theory in so far as further describing the role of the Scientist of Consciousness in the exploration of the nonphysical reality, the following chapter detailing the rise of the New Science will present a much more detailed analysis. Bear with us for just a few pages as I discuss my Teaching in broad strokes, for what we have termed "our general audience." A moment...

Now for your information, Dear Reader, your world is composed entirely of thought. A musician composes musical works of art with notes as the creative material. In the creation of realities, the human in the Third Dimension uses thought in artistic ways. To carry the comparison further... just as the "mad" artist might refuse to admit their creation of the art before them - paintings, let us say - the majority of human beings refuse to admit that they have had a hand in the <u>literal</u> creation of their physical world. Certainly many of you would say that this is crazy thinking, or "magical thinking" as your psychiatrists refer to it. You have become so estranged from your works that you fail to see yourselves in the "mirror" of your physical reality.

Unconscious Creation

One reason for this estrangement is that this creation of your world is done largely on the unconscious level. It is truly a projection, in this sense, for you are individually projecting your subconscious thoughts, images and other mental constructs out onto the "screen" of your Personal Reality Field.

Your thoughts give birth to realities. Fearful thoughts give birth to fearful realities. Thoughts of Courage and Loving Understanding give birth to Courageous and Loving realities. You may witness this for yourself within your own manifestations. Watch and see how each element in

16

your perceptual field REFLECTS your inner state of emotion and imagination.

Example - Unconscious Creation

Let us present an example here for illustration. Imagine if you will, a human undergoing an extremely stressful life event. Perhaps this person has incurred a job loss and is quite worried about the financial implications of this negative event. The emotional state of this human is chaotic - stress-filled - as a cascade of Negative Emotions floods their mental environment. Consequently, the Personal Reality Field of this person is also chaotic. And because it is created from Negative Emotions, there are numerous triggers within their Personal Reality radius that "cause," in a reflexive fashion, the continuing recreation of Negative Emotions within their psyche.

Now immediately prior to the job loss, let us say that the mental environment of this human was quite balanced and even "happy." Their monetary needs were met. Their needs for a social outlet were met with the job as well. So the firing of this person had a devastating effect upon their mental stability, as you may well imagine.

Now let us further propose that a great mistake was made here with this firing of our theoretical worker. The employer made a mistake through a mix-up of some sort, and upon discovering this, they immediately rectified the error, by perhaps calling the hapless human and giving them their job back. Well, again as you can imagine, the Personal Reality

Field of this human example was instantly transformed with the call from the employer reinstating them in their position. Happiness was again experienced. Relief from monetary worry was experienced, as well as gratitude, perhaps, that they would continue to enjoy the social amenities of their employment with humans with whom they had developed strong, Loving relationships.

I hope you see my point here in this example. You are all, as humans existing within the Third Dimension, engaged in a witnessing of your mental environments projected outward into physical reality on a moment-to-moment basis. The ideas and images within your psyches are the blueprints for the creation of the varied Reality Constructs that compose your Personal Reality Field. The mutable emotions are the energies that power this Reality Creation phenomenon.

Central Field of Experiencing

Let me add to this cursory explanation with a description of a new metaphor we are presenting: the Central Field of Experiencing. Now you exist within an intersection of dimensional planes. If I may, I would like to enlist Mark's skills as an illustrator to create for you a graphic representation of this dimensional intersection. *(Seth presented an image to my mental environment. See my rendering on the next page. mf)*

The illustration shows the intersection of several planes. They share a common area, as you can see, that we shall call

CENTRAL FIELD OF EXPERIENCING

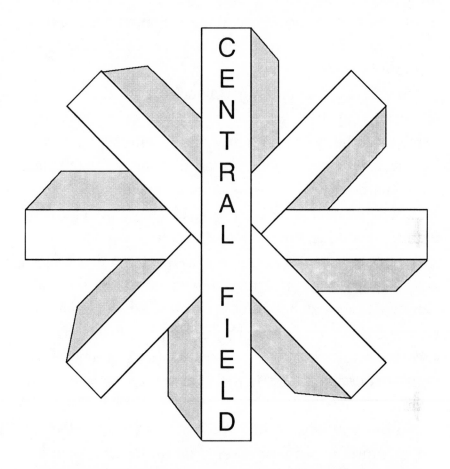

YOU LIVE MANY LIVES SIMULTANEOUSLY. THE CENTRAL FIELD
OF EXPERIENCING REPRESENTS YOUR CURRENT EXISTENCE
IN THIRD-DIMENSIONAL REALITY. THE INTERSECTING PLANES
REPRESENT YOUR OTHER LIVES LIVED WITHIN PAST, PRESENT
AND FUTURE TIMEFRAMES, ON EARTH, IN OTHER SYSTEMS
AND IN PROBABLE REALITIES. YOU HAVE THE POTENTIAL TO
EXPERIENCE THE EVENTS OCCURRING WITHIN ALL OF YOUR
OTHER LIVES FROM WITHIN YOUR CURRENT EXISTENCE.

~ SETH

your Central Field of Experiencing. Let us say that each of these planes of existence represents one of your Simultaneous Lives. Let us further state that the common area here, your Central Field, is your current self experiencing life in this timeframe.

Now all of these planes are connected at the Central Field, and so not only does your current self have at its disposal the perceptual ability to experience events within your current life, but also, because you are indeed connected to the other lives - hard-wired, in a sense - you have the POTENTIAL to experience events, feel emotions and have thoughts from within these other simultaneously-lived lives.

The planes surrounding the Central Field represent your various Reincarnational Selves as well as the many PROBABLE existences that you co-create with your consciousness and All That Is. This Central Field, then, is your current Third-Dimensional existence. Look around you at your surroundings. This is what we are referring to in this current discussion.

Now as you look around you what do you see? Do you see a futuristic landscape with mythological creatures grazing on the lawn? Do you see a vignette of interaction between two family members from a life in a Mystery Civilization, such as Atlantis? Do you witness the life you are living now, complete in every detail except for one? Perhaps there is a stranger, someone you do not recognize, apparently living their life with you in your home. Does this unique detail "prove" to you that you are viewing a scene that does not exist in your current physical reality?

I would guess that you are perceiving your surroundings as quite similar to those you left behind you as you proceeded to read this book. My point here is that the possibility exists for you, in this time of accelerated consciousness, during this Dimensional-Shift we have described to you in our new books, to briefly inhabit the bodies of your Reincarnational Selves. You accomplish this by refocusing your perceptive apparatus - the Inner Senses - on a tangential plane of existence. You will be picking up on the sensory experiencing of these humans who are indeed you, Dear Reader, as you are engaged in living your lives within the many timeframes on your Earth and in other systems.

Example - Tuning-In to Other Lives

For example: if my friend Mark was to select at random one of the planes surrounding the Central Field of Experiencing in our diagram, and using his imagination and his Inner Senses "tuned-in" to another life, he might very well find himself experiencing his aboriginal existence, or possibly his existence as a female in New Orleans Louisiana in the U.S.A. or as a Roman soldier from many hundreds of years ago, in your terms. These are just a few of Mark's Reincarnational Existences.

You Dear Reader also have a vast store of existences just waiting to be explored. This illustration may serve as a meditation piece for you in this way. In each of our books in this series, we have presented these simple focusing tools to assist you in perceiving your greater reality - the reality of your Soul Self. Please utilize this tool in your experimentation as you attempt to access your other lives.

The Emotional Body

Please focus on the illustration on the next page. In the center of this drawing we have identified a theoretical structure we will call The Emotional Body. This Emotional Body may be perceived as the intersection of "energies" of Reality Creation within your physical body construct. You may experience it as existing within the heart region. It is within this construct that the Reality Creation agendas of ALL of your Reincarnational Existences may be read. You may, for example, observe within this Emotional Body the emotional and symbolic underpinnings of a chronic illness that currently plagues you. *(See Chapter Six. mf)* Or you may witness a dramatization of an event from your past that keeps you from enjoying prosperity in your present. *(See Chapter Seven. mf)* Thus you may sense these strategies in your own particular fashion, using the Inner Senses that you are developing through experimentation in this project.

The greater sphere of activity within which rests this Emotional Body we refer to as The Light Body, as do many of the current teachers and practitioners in your world. This construct is "built" from the intersecting energies of existence - or dimensions if you prefer - of your many

THE LIGHT BODY

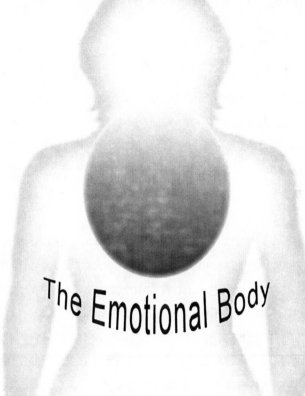

The Emotional Body

The Light Body is the sum of your Simultaneous Lives expressed through your physical body. The Emotional Body may be visualized as an oval Energy Form suspended within the heart region. The Auric Vision is the Inner Senses reading of issues and remedies expressed within the Emotional Body. -- Seth

Simultaneous Lives. This Inner Senses representation of The Emotional Body, as well as the Inner Sense of sight itself, we are calling the Auric Vision...

Now please allow me to digress a moment on my choice of words and phrases...

Choice of Terms

I realize that these are words that may carry their own emotional undertones for you the reader. I would ask you, then, if this is the case, to look beyond the ego-identified definitions and references of these terms. Although it is not my desire to challenge you excessively in this endeavor, challenge you I must. As an educator to humanity for "countless" years, in your terms, I have found it advantageous to present material for the student's assessment that stands what you might call "diametrically opposed" to the ideas, images and beliefs that the student may be holding in their mental environment at any one time. I do hope that, if you feel rising anger and righteous indignation making itself known within - as I have just described to you - The Emotional Body, that you perhaps take a deep breath and go deeper with this work of ours, this project yours and mine.

You see, the Soul's perspective is necessarily <u>through</u> the ego/intellect. I would suggest, in times of anger and when feeling affronted by this material, you simply step to the side a bit, metaphorically speaking, and allow your Soul Self to perceive your world. This is an easy first step in the "awakening" process. Please have faith, or perhaps Courage is a better word here, that this project will pay off for you in many different ways, rewarding you with information of a decidedly beneficial nature.

Body of Light

Now this Emotional Body is perceived as Light to the Inner Senses. It is also conceived in Light. All is Light. Everything in your created reality is composed of Light in the form of our theoretical constructs the Consciousness Units. Here we are simplifying and spiritualizing my messages to humanity. For this reason we shall also refer to the Energy Construct of the human physical body as being composed of spiritual information.

In this context, you Dear Reader, are a divine message from All That Is, articulating your particular philosophy, behaviors and mentality within physical reality as an "envoy" of the sacred. Again, if you are tempted to dismiss this as mere "religious ranting," I urge you to take a deep breath and go within for just a moment. Sense your ultimate divinity. It is obvious to we who are now instructing you, the nonphysical beings, and to you it may become obvious in your experimentation, as you discover Findings that support my statement.

Personal Reality Field

The Inner Senses, the nonphysical counterparts to your outer physical senses, are the creators of your Personal

Reality Field. Perception creates reality in your Third Dimension. And the reality you create is dependent wholly upon what you <u>believe</u> is possible. If you are experiencing a reality of peace and Loving Understanding with your fellow inhabitants of Earth, you have a system of beliefs that permits, allows and effectively determines a Personal Reality Field of peace and Loving Understanding. You have in this example, believed into existence your peaceful Loving world.

Now it is also true that <u>everything</u> you find in your Personal Reality Field you have <u>believed</u> into reality. Might I say that, for the most part, if you feel uncomfortable, fearful, anxious with the state of your Personal Reality, it may be due to your creating unconsciously? Creating unconsciously leaves you open to the Negative Entities. Watch your thoughts. Watch where your fearful thoughts originate. Are they being amplified and corroborated within the negative spheres of influence?

The negative realms are sensed as separate from self. The Negative Entities that reside within these spheres of activity normally will not seek you out and attempt to fix on your being. Yet if you are experiencing negative, anxious, angry, or violent emotional states, you leave yourself open to encountering these influences. For this reason, it is important to observe your emotional states throughout your waking reality. If you are experiencing fear, assess your sensing and Reality Creation and see if you are being driven by negative outside sources.

Yet please rest assured that if you find yourself "contaminated" by these energies, you may easily correct your situation. You may do so with your Intention in the moment. What I would suggest you do is first perform the experiment we have called Clearing The Emotional Body. *(From Book Two. mf)* This activity raises the Negative Emotions from the emotional center to the mental center where they may be transformed into their opposites.

Briefly, you simply relax in a meditative posture and imagine or visualize the "churning" energies of The Emotional Body rising up to the mental center directly between your physical eyes. Emotional resolution is achieved. The contact with the Divine is established. See the end of this chapter for a means to create this state long term.

Beliefs and the Shift

Your feedback reality continually endorses your ongoing emotional states according to the "structures" of your beliefs. Here we shall define beliefs as those "habitual patterns of perceptual analysis utilized in the creation of Reality Constructs." Your beliefs are the potent ideas, images and emotional contents that exist within your mental environment or psyche. Your beliefs may be thought of as the "rough sketch" for your creative project - your ongoing life with its experiences, behaviors, and so on.

Now currently it is possible for you to address issues of core beliefs and core values, like never before in your history as a species. Your evolution as a Soul depends upon a fundamental change in your beliefs. You will not, individually or collectively, make the transition we have been discussing in these new manuscripts with the outmoded beliefs you currently hold.

The world is integrating, you see, at an extremely rapid pace. You in the developed nations, the many millions of you, are behind the learning curve in this matter. This may be due to your obsession with material objects of mass consumption. The prevalence of the egoic perspective within your individual and mass consciousness also holds you back. And it certainly does not serve you in the West to "export" these limited perspectives through your Negative Media and through your military excursions into foreign lands.

This is why I am again writing books, you see. The greater part of the world is awakening "on schedule." It is in the developed nations in particular, and some other parts of your world, that you are still focused on the creation of negative, fear-based realities.

Lessons and the Shift

Now this "quickening" is indeed upon you in Third-Dimensional Reality. Those of you engaged in negative ruminations, and their attendant manifestation into negative Reality Constructs, will find that you are confronted, in an almost simultaneous fashion, with the products of your mental digressions. Just as the practitioners of Loving Understanding and Courage will find their positive manifestations strengthening, so too will the practitioners of doubt, anger, hatred and such, find themselves consumed with the energies released during these errant creative activities.

Is there any wonder why such an intensification of this creative process produces the appropriate results? You create your own reality according to your beliefs. If you are focusing on the fear and cynical distrust of your neighbors, for example, is it any wonder that your neighbors continue to cause you discomfort? And is it any wonder that as you awaken as a species this discomfort grows? Indeed, I suggest the discomfort may grow until it becomes UNBEARABLE. Then you will of necessity be faced with a choice in your reincarnational dramas. Will you learn your Lesson or will you not? Will you continue to hold-on to the anger, fear and cynicism, or will you let-go and feel the ecstasy just below the surface of your human consciousness? This ecstasy is the creative Loving energy of All That Is.

Free Will and Divine Will

Your choice in these matters IS a matter of your free will in the moment. Might I suggest that in these moments of opportunity for You the Soul, that you listen to the suggestions of your Guides rather than to the self-centered voice of the ego/intellect? This is merely a suggestion, my friend. The free will choice is yours and I am acting here in a purely advisory capacity. (humorously) I simply urge you to take your own advice in these situations, when in fact you are embodying the Soul Self. It will be quite easy to determine if you are experiencing this unique perspective. The Soul Self is informed through communications with All That Is. This perspective may guide you to the best resolution of any given creative challenge you may face.

The differences between the subconscious creation of negative realities and the conscious co-creation of positive, life-affirming realities by the awakening human consciousness through use of the Divine Will are quite pronounced. *(See Chapter Six. mf)* You will know it when you sense it. You will recognize the differences when you are faced with a decision to go one way or the other. I will leave it at that for now. Obviously, you are each required to learn your individual Lessons. I would not wish to give you ALL the answers, and by so doing, rob you of the "joy" of learning your Lessons on your own. (humorously)

Belief Change

Now there are at least two distinct ways to go with regards to belief change, if you do indeed wish to change your beliefs and thus your reality: you may change your perceptions of your Personal Reality Field, or you can go for direct change of the underlying beliefs themselves. I have covered this in *The Nature of Personal Reality*, and I will now update that information for my current Teaching in this new readership we are addressing. First, through the ancient technologies of Healing Talk via the Trance State, and through other Rituals of Contact and Communication with nonphysical beings, *(See Chapter Six. mf)* such as the Energy Personality and other Energy Bodies, the perceptions of the Personal Reality may be altered, thus altering the Reality Creation. We may also describe this as a "fine tuning" of the Inner Senses, so that they may more clearly perceive and create.

The second method entails identifying the beliefs you wish to change through a self-questioning process and creating more productive belief statements representing improved "healthier" beliefs that you wish to "make your own." The statements are then continuously written down or typed into a computer, the theory being that the new beliefs are internalized the more that you document them.

These two methods represent two different ways of relating to physical reality: the imaginal and the literal. Naturally there are others. If you feel more comfortable visualizing your beliefs, I suggest you use the imaginal method in your experiments. If you feel more comfortable writing them down, use the literal approach. And of course, beyond my humble offerings, use your own methods that suit you.

Again, for those of you who may feel uncomfortable with terms such as Trance State and Rituals of Contact and Communication, please make up your own names for these states of consciousness. I am merely using common terms that the majority of my readers may understand. And please remember, that it was through the studied use of the Trance State that these communications first began and do indeed continue. With the person you know as Jane Roberts, it was a delicate dance of consciousness that we engaged in to create the appropriate environment

31

for our collaboration. The Trance State is used by many of us on the subtle levels as we attempt to make ourselves understood to those of you in the Third Dimension.

As for our use of the term Ritual to describe the process of contacting and communicating with the denizens of nonphysical reality, please note that the term Ritual is the precise one used in your World Religions to describe their individual and varied methods for contacting the various spirits, gods and goddesses, God, and what have you. So we are merely presenting terms already in common usage by those of you in the West and elsewhere. Your experiment for this chapter follows.

Experiment - The Divine Day
Hypothesis: you may create contact with the divine over the course of an entire waking day.

This experiment is one of creating the Trance State long term. For our purposes, the Trance is a sacred state of awareness. When you conduct your Ritual of Sanctuary and enter your Trance, you are walking the Path of the seeker of wisdom. When you can embody this state of awareness over the course of minutes and hours, you will be well on your way toward awakening to the Unity of Consciousness Dimension that we have described in our new books.

Now choose a day when you will not be bothered by outside forces. You will want to be left alone for this experiment, if at all possible. We are assuming here that you have already experienced some form of contact and communication with one or more of your Guides. However, if you have yet to manifest this relationship, simply "act as if" you are already in touch with your Energy Personality. Conduct this experiment as though guided by your Spirit Guide, for this may well act to initiate that relationship.

In my last book I presented an exercise in bringing the energy of Reality Creation up from the emotional center into the mental center. This mental center is located directly between your eyes. It is here that you may sense the divine information stream as it seeks to penetrate the barrier of the ego/intellect. Just as we encourage the users of The Healing Regimen to create the healing moment long term - into minutes, hours and days *(See Chapter Six. mf)* - we encourage you the reader to create this initial contemplative state for as long as you can. It would be best if you could begin the Divine Day on awakening from sleep.

Perform your Ritual of Sanctuary

If you have yet to develop your Ritual of Sanctuary, simply imagine a golden Light surrounding you. Nothing harmful can penetrate this field of Light. It has a healing protective influence.

Now create the Trance State as best you can. The Trance is simply a natural state of awareness marked by deep relaxation and a focus on the inner world. I would ask you to sense what energies may be present in the solar plexus area of your body. If you sense a churning activity, as though emotions were ebbing and flowing, please bring this felt sense UP to the mental center directly between your eyes. As you do this exercise, you may notice that the churning sensation ceases. The felt sense becomes one of calm and assurance. There is also an emotional tone of ecstasy just below the surface. This is an indication that you are using your Intent to bring it up, up into the divine portal.

Findings - Document throughout your waking day your experiences with keeping your awareness in the mental center.

The Divine Day

Date: _____

_____

_____

_____

_____

_____

_____

_____

_____

_____

_____

_____

CHAPTER THREE

The New Science

Dialogue - Chaos
9/21/06 12:48 PM

Mark: Everything seems to be falling apart. Any comments?
Seth: Yes, have the faith and Courage that can see you through this TEMPORARY situation. Chaos is the order of the day. All is in flux. Now a positive spin on this state of affairs might be, "from chaos, all is made." You must deconstruct the status quo before you can begin to rebuild your reality with Light - the Love Light of All That Is.
Do you remember?
Mark: I do now.
Seth: Then let us continue...

The New Science

Currently there is an interesting phenomenon you may have noticed in your communities. Others are creating their own names for this development. We are calling it the growth of the New Science. This New Science we have named "new," not because it is anything new. After all, it is merely the reformation of collective wisdom that you have forgotten. But to your traditional scientists and to those of you who are just learning of these subjects, it does indeed appear to be new, to be novel.

This New Science I speak of is rising up within your group consciousness as a dream does, in that you may immediately sense the power and truth within its postulates. It is a response on the part of your Mother Earth and All That Is to the isolation of the human consciousness, within the vast cold and spiritless mental environment of the Old Science.

Authorities

The New Science represents a rebirth of essentially revolutionary material. As such, these ideas and images, as they are made known within the collective awareness, will be met with resistance and denial by those in authority. The authority in your modern world is all powerful. YOU have empowered the authority with your valuable Reality Creation energies while denying your own powers to create your world. Only the scientist, the priest, the politician knows what is best for you. Am I right? (humorously) For this reason, the New Science will be met with disdain, cynicism, fear. Just as the witches and other practitioners of the Divine were destroyed in your perceived past, the current authorities resident in your social, political and religious hierarchies will attempt to destroy the practitioners of the New Science.

Let me say here that some of my readers may have a built-in prejudice with regards to this renaissance of creative thought. You are reluctant to pursue these explorations for you have been punished, often severely, in your Reincarnational Existences for practicing these arcane arts. As I have recently described to participants in one of our public forums, it is quite possible that those of you who are seeking out my material, have "met your maker" at the hands of the authorities in what you might refer to as "past lives." And so you are reluctant to "tempt fate," as it were, and perhaps incur the wrath of the local magistrate or religious official.

Protoscientists

The modern scientific tradition is giving way to a body of work that was created by the forebears of your world. These protoscientists lived within the Mystery Civilizations. We refer to these as Mystery Civilizations for the obvious reason that you have forgotten the valuable insights into human behavior and the nature of reality that you learned within these societies.

I have described to you how mankind has ceded the powers of Reality Creation to those in authority in exchange for "subtle gifts" - the protection of the group, the opportunity to earn a living, the confirmation of a place in the hereafter etc.; etc.; etc. This giving-up of power went hand-in-hand with a mass forgetting of the old traditions of healing, group spirituality and wonder-workings of various kinds.

Precept and Percept

I have returned to remind you of these forgotten facts of your existence. These are the **precepts** - a word I coined with my First Subject - that when fully understood, will allow you to witness and remember the activities of your Simultaneous Lives, for example, as well as the literal moment-to-moment creation of your Personal Reality from the thoughts and images within your mental environment.

Examples of precepts:

You create your own reality.

You are connected to everything in your world.

You can change the Consensus Reality from your Personal Reality Field.

Emotion is the creative energy of All That Is in action.

Human consciousness is founded in Love.

Diversions from Love through Negative Emotions create Negative Realities.

All imbalances may be corrected through Love and Courage.

You are the sum of your Simultaneous Lives within your current Moment Point.

Your Inner Senses may be used to examine and change anything past, present or future.

You are in telepathic rapport with everything in your world.

Reality Constructs are composed of Consciousness Units of awarized energy.

Coordinate Points permeate matter and space and modulate the activity of the Consciousness Units.
Your Intention, Emotions and Beliefs provide the energy and direction for Reality Creation.
Everything exists initially as Gestalts of Consciousness, the nonphysical "templates" of creation.

Now the **percept** here - a slightly different spelling than precept, I trust you shall notice - is another very important concept we shall discuss. We are redefining this term in the New Science. *(See Q&A on Whitehead. Whitehead used the term in his writings. mf)* A percept may be defined as, "that element of consciousness that creates the Reality Construct and instantaneously perceives or witnesses the construct."

Let us discuss some of these ideas in greater depth. All of this will be accomplished, I sincerely hope (humorously), with an eye toward "unpacking" the theory supporting this New Science.

Subconscious Thought

To reiterate, your world is largely created by subconscious thought, as you know. During the dreamstate you create incipient Reality Constructs that you materialize into physical Reality Constructs on awakening. Now it may already seem obvious to you that you create your physical body without much <u>conscious</u> thought. Your unconscious, in tandem with All That Is, creates your physical body "naturally," without the need for constant energy or direction from the conscious mind or ego. However, as we explore the expression of the Soul <u>through</u> the ego, and you begin to correct your negative thoughts and their expression into physical Reality Constructs, you will begin to gain conscious control of these unconscious processes. This is the path of healing the physical body, for example. You learn how to fine-tune the expression of Consciousness Units through the Coordinate Points for the creation of an improved or symptom-free body. *(See Chapter Six. mf)*

Consciousness Units

These Consciousness Units are, of course, the ubiquitous elements of awarized energy - the "building blocks" of Reality Creation - that we spoke of in our last book. And as for the Coordinate Points... some of you may remember this concept of mine that I first delineated in **Seth Speaks**. Here we shall simplify the Idea Construct for dissemination to a broader audience. To begin, I am sending Mark a hologram to illustrate the expression of Coordinate Point and CU activity within his physical body. This will serve as a theoretical AND practical basis for Mark to find success in the creation of physical health within his Personal Reality.

(I experienced the hologram as an influx of ecstatic energy, reminding me that I may use the Loving assistance of All That Is to heal myself of the difficulties that I am

currently experiencing. By avoiding this knowledge as I prepared the second book, I contracted an illness and became quite disabled. I was very concerned that I would make my Transition in my 50s, just as Jane Roberts had done. mf)

The Coordinate Points permeate your Third-Dimensional Reality and direct the "activity" of the CUs, according to the energy templates of Gestalts of Consciousness. You could say that the potential for physical expression of the CU is "adjusted" by the CP at the direction of subconscious and conscious thought.

Now need I mention that this is a collective effort? The creation of your world is an exercise in mutual cooperation between your "human" consciousness and the "creative intelligence" or consciousness of everything else in your world. This description pertains to the greater as well as the lesser here. You cooperate with every atom within your Personal Reality Field as well as every atom within the greater reality field that you might call your Consensus Reality.

Coordinate Points and Reality Creation

Some areas of your world hold "more" of the Coordinate Points than others. These parts of your planet are much desired as places of worship and meditation. The potentialities for manifestation into physical reality are greater in these areas of high energy or accelerated vibration. Yet within your own personal environment, you

41

may find with just a bit of exploration, just where the processes of creation work best for you.

For example: have you ever found that the simple act of changing your study location within your home had the effect of greatly streamlining the creative process for you? Perhaps intuitively you understood that the dispersal of Coordinate Points in the new area was more conducive to study and learning than the previous one.

The Coordinate Points may also be conceived of as gateways into adjacent dimensions representing different timeframes and so different Reincarnational Existences. I hope I am not complicating this discussion too much with these heady topics and definitions. Later on in this manuscript we shall go further into our explanations with examples and experimentation.

For now let us just say that the precept - for example, "you create your own reality" - may be thought of as the general, overriding influence in this New Science theory, while as I said, the percept may represent the "cutting edge" - a useful comparison - of consciousness as it creates and perceives the world.

Science of the Sacred

The activity of the Consciousness Unit via the Coordinate Point is spontaneous, that is, the creative energies "erupt" into the Reality Constructs within your field of perception, in a milieu of Loving ease and divine facilitation. This spontaneity I am describing is based in the Divine, yet naturally the outcomes of these activities are witnessed in the physical - your physical world. You straddle both the etheric and the physical domains.

This New Science we are describing is not separate from the sacred. It is an analysis OF the sacred. The sacred here is the subject of study. The sacred is the spinning of Consciousness Units into Reality Constructs by All That Is through you the reader of this book. Here I use the term "spinning" in a multitude of ways. Your essence is spun off of All That Is in the manner of a top as it spins, casting off a flash of reflected light, perhaps, the flash of light representing a fragment of the Soul Self that is cast into the living body of the human baby. I am also referencing the spinning of your theoretical electrons in your atoms.

Happy Atoms

My friend Mark here is quite fond of our concept of Love Light, and so I shall elaborate on this metaphor for his benefit as well as yours, Dear Reader. Now the elements you know as atoms are Loving and benign entities. In terms of what we might call a "generic" atom, within the activity of creation in the New Science theory, the sole goal of the atom is to combine creatively with other atoms in experiencing Value Fulfillment.

Now certainly you might question whether an atom could have an agenda or could think or in any way assess its existence in the fulfillment of value. Let me remind you that everything is alive. Everything is sentient, self-reflective to a degree. Even an atom may be thought of as having a strategy for development. The atoms and the Consciousness Units of which they are composed, have strategies for the fulfillment of particular values.

Love

Building upon this premise, can you see how a natural trajectory for a "typical" Consciousness Unit or atom might well be toward the creation of Love? Love is information or light. What I shall be referring to as Love Light in this manuscript, then, is simply information of a particular type. It is the creative force of manifestation.

If you have been following our discussion of the nature of reality, you will remember that I have described All That Is as the source for ALL realities. You may then see that it follows that Love in our model of Reality Creation, is the energy or "impetus" for the expression of All That Is within your Third Dimension.

This is not new information I am providing to humanity. Your World Religions place great importance on the role of Love within society. The virtues of Love are spoken of by many healers and leaders within your communities. Yet here I hope to define what I am calling "Love with a capital L." The Love that I am describing to you is the literal "fuel" for the manifestation of EVERYTHING in your world. This Love or Love Light has a particular frequency or rate of vibration that facilitates the assemblage of Consciousness Units into Reality Constructs. The Love Light is the power of All That Is. Period. It is the force that activates the CUs to express ideas and images into physical reality through the Coordinate Points. Do you see, then, that it is important to learn how to utilize this Love Light in a conscious deliberate fashion?

However, you might well ask, "But Seth, where is the Love currently? My world is certainly lacking in the Love that creates realities!" We shall have more to say on the diversion of Love in the creation of negative realities later in this manuscript. For now, please remember that your Earth is a dramatic stage for the enactment of what are often perceived as "negative" or "painful" reincarnational dramas. *(See Chapter Eight. mf)*

These dramas may indeed "appear" to be devoid of Love in any measure. However, you have "set yourself up" to experience your Lessons in the way you are experiencing them. Indeed, your ultimate Lesson in the Third Dimension may be the learning of how to use your formidable energies of creation to create the positive out of the negative. Coincidentally, that is the precise subject of this book. (humorously)

Love Light Matrix and Metaphors

The Love Light is the matrix of divine influences onto which you fashion your Reality Constructs. Here let us speak of the importance of context. It is ALL context, Dear Reader. Within this milieu we are describing as the Love Light Matrix, the Telepathic Network, the Central

Field of Experiencing and the Subconscious Manifestation Energy Stream, you create out of Consciousness Units those Reality Constructs that compose what you experience as "bedrock reality"- a cliché we have found helpful in these discussions.

Of course we use metaphors in this work to assist the reader in an understanding of the principles and ideas we are describing. Again, the creation of your Personal Reality Field that you accomplish on a moment-to-moment basis with the divine energy of All That Is, is so complex an undertaking that your physical brain could not conceive of the many operations that are undergone within ONE SINGLE SECOND of your existence.

Mark, my Third Subject in this lineage of collaboration, has a term he uses, a carry over from his days as a flower child - "mind blower." This refers to, I gather, a concept or image that is so stunning that a single human mind cannot comprehend it in its totality. This is an apt description of what the mind encounters when these matters of Reality Creation are considered.

To express the Divine - the ineffable - we must always resort to metaphors and theoretical constructs, for the reality of the subject matter is so incredibly complex and rich, that the Third-Dimensional consciousness cannot hold it for very long before it falls away into chaos. The great traditions of your world teach the student how to maintain an equilibrium in these matters. The hope is that the student will master the skills of witnessing the Divine without succumbing to the negative states of fear, anger, confusion. So metaphors are used.

Now perhaps some mixing of metaphors is necessary here to provide a choice for you the reader. (humorously) We are hoping that you will find some image or idea that works for you here in the understanding of this material. We are preparing you for the regimens that follow these introductory chapters.

Threads, Strands and Gestalts of Consciousness

In my book on Soul Evolution, I described the Consciousness Units as being composed of threads. I now further state that these theoretical threads of awarized energy exist in various "arrays" of potentiality, what we are calling Gestalts of Consciousness - the premanifestation templates of creation. Infinitesimally small threads of energy under the direction of your human mentality, and also under the direction of elemental consciousness, coalesce into strands of incipient matter that are combined in various ways to create your Reality Constructs.

Now a matrix implies a grid or network of interconnecting pathways or energy streams. Can you imagine in your mind's eye this network of Love Light? The pathways are the strands of etheric material composed of CUs. Within this matrix exist the Coordinate Points. The strands also coalesce into more complex structures - the Gestalts of Consciousness - which hold the potential for the creation of anything conceived by consciousness. All of this etheric material is literally "Love in action" - the all-encompassing power of Love that is the essence and creative energy of All That Is.

Are you beginning to see now? This Love Light energy that powers the strands of etheric material, is the creative element for healing of all types. Focused Love Light is utilized by your tribal healers, for example, in very precise ways to assist their "patients" in balancing and "making whole" their unbalanced bodies. So it is literally true that Love is the healing agent in all restorations of the human body and spirit.

Subconscious Manifestation Energy Stream

Now the strands of incipient matter we have just discussed compose the latticework that is the grid of Coordinate Points upon and within and about your self-created reality. I am attempting to send Mark a hologram to illustrate this last statement of mine.

(He was successful. It was a brief image reminiscent of the work of Alex Gray, the New Age artist of human energy. mf)

What I hoped to convey to Mark was the all-inclusive holographic nature of these strands of incipient matter. They compose the physical Reality Constructs of your Third-Dimensional world INCLUDING your own physical body and the physical constructs that you might call space, air etc.

So can you now imagine, as I attempt to bring this description to fullness, how this Reality Construction phenomenon might exist as a profound image? Can you imagine the creation of Third-Dimensional Reality in its totality as being powered or energized into activity? What is lacking here in our description, you see, is the motivating energizing power that sustains the phenomenon. A moment... let us refer to this concept as the Subconscious Manifestation Energy Stream. This energy flow supports your reality by continuously lending the creative energy of All That Is to the manifestation of each and every construct in your Personal Reality Field.

The SMES is subconscious. It is driven by your Soul's Intent. You are experiencing on Earth your reincarnational dramas and comedies to further the education of your Soul Self. This subconscious Intent is other-directed. It is directed in essence by All That Is. Now you decided before you were born, what body you were to inhabit and what Lessons you were to learn in this current life. So you truly do co-create with All That Is your Earthly existence. But again I must remind you that you have free will "to do as you please," even while in the midst of your Lessons, which might be of a truly sober and serious nature.

Auric Vision

As I described to you in Book Two, each atom in your perceptive field exists within its own electromagnetic energy environment or Auric Field. Each and every Reality Construct also rests within its own Auric Field. With your Inner Sense of Auric Vision, you may easily perceive this "visual" aspect of your self-created physical objects.

The advantage to using this Inner Sense as opposed to say the physical outer sense of sight may not be obvious at first. Let me explain. The electromagnetic corona reveals information about not merely the Reality Construct or physical object itself, but about the individual atoms or CU's of which it is composed. Each atom has its own evolutionary history, you see, and each atom retains and "exhibits" not only "past" historic data but also "future" information to the observer.

We have discussed elsewhere in these writings that each atom or CU in the Universe is connected to every other atom or CU in the created Universe. Additionally, each CU or atom retains its own history. For example: any particular atom might have a history of, let us say, existing as a molecule of water that was incorporated into a plant, that was then, as an addition to the cellular tissue of the plant, eaten by an animal. The animal incorporated the plant material into its flesh. Now the water molecule is transformed, in this example, into plant cell and then into animal flesh. Yet the molecule or atom or CU of water we are describing RETAINS what we might call the "memories" of its existence as part of a water molecule, a plant cell and the flesh of an animal.

Now if you, again as an example, were to eat the flesh of this theoretical beast we are describing, and you incorporated the atom that is journeying from construct to construct, even then this atom would retain memories of its existence in the preceding constructs. Each CU, each atom, each cell that composes your physical body here in this example, has a cellular history that it, in a sense, "remembers," and one that is reflected within the Auric Field or corona of our human example, in this case, you the reader of this book.

This plodding explanation, I think, is necessary for your understanding of this Inner Sense we are calling Auric Vision. Do you see how the atoms of the body literally sing their histories in unison with one another? These "songs" are the electromagnetic vibrations that may be sensed as the Auric Field.

Now these Inner Senses blend into each other somewhat and so we may speak of the Inner Sense of sight as having an auditory component also. The inner eye senses the Auric field as, in a manner of speaking, the inner ear senses the vibrations or songs of the collected cells of the energy construct - the human body, your body.

The atoms "sing" their histories as well as their present and future realities. The electromagnetic expressions of individual atoms or CUs, as well as the collective expressions of your self-created Reality Constructs, display for the keen observer the mysteries of creation. You are all psychics, you see. All of you have the potential to become wonder workers, with the simple acknowledgment that you, by virtue of your simple humanity, have the potential for discovering the Inner Senses. With this discovery comes the real possibility for spiritual growth.

This Subconscious Manifestation Energy Stream is the energetic construct - or holographic model, if you prefer - for the creation and maintenance of your Personal Reality Field, and by association the Consensus Reality Field. For the Consensus Reality is the sum of the Personal Reality Fields of a given area.

Making Breakfast

I would very much like to complete this description with an example of a typical act of manifestation, one you may be familiar with as an eater of breakfast. A moment...

(Seth is relating this to some dictation he transmitted through Cas in my office several years ago. mf)

You the reader of this book have possibly experienced the phenomenon of "making" your own breakfast. Let me just say that this is the perfect word for this process of creation. For you not only "make" your breakfast, in the sense that you prepare the various elements of the meal, "the way you like it," and put them on the plate, but you literally create - through a type of "telepathic rapport" with the atomic structures of the various elements - the foods contained in the meal.

I do like the term telepathic rapport. It describes quite nicely this sense of collaboration with all of the energies within your Personal Reality Field. You are ONE with all of the CUs within your Personal Reality Field and you give direction to these elements to create your realities. This rapport may also be described as "attunement" - an ongoing correlation between your human Intuition and the countless atoms that comprise any particular event in your life. Let us now complete this section of our book with some experimentation that will hopefully illustrate for you the principles we have just discussed.

Prelude to Sensing Reality Creation

Dear Reader, you now have at your disposal the great perceptive powers of the Inner Senses. In my last book I described to you in detail how to access these powers and how to use them to your advantage in physical reality. Here I would like to elaborate on this data with some suggestions on how to sense the Subconscious Manifestation Energy Stream.

Mark, this material may also be used in conjunction with the Jung material. *(Seth is writing a book on the post-Transition reality of Carl Jung. mf)* The Subconscious Manifestation Energy Stream, as I said, supports and nourishes your created reality - your Personal Reality Field. In the dream state, and when you are in your Home Dimension between lives, you are well aware of this stream of energy and you sense it as easily as you sense the various constructs within your self-created reality. Now, the Inner Sense of sight, Auric Vision, may be utilized to sense this stream. The following experiment will assist you in the awakening of this valuable Inner Sense.

Experiment - Sensing Reality Creation
Hypothesis: the smes may be observed as it creates the reality construct.

The Reality Construct is our topic for the moment. The Reality Construct is all of created reality, and it also describes the many elements of the created reality. Here I wish to digress somewhat and ask you the reader to imagine for yourself what it is I am attempting to describe to you.

Consciousness creates form, instantaneously, in the moment. We must use these descriptions of Reality Creation for you to make sense of this phenomenon, occurring as it does within a linear time conceptualization. The truth of the matter might be better expressed by describing the spontaneously <u>responsive</u> quality of manifestation in your system. So that here you could speak of consciousness creating form that creates consciousness, and so on, all within the spacious eternal moment. Everything is conscious. Everything is creative. Everything creates consciousness. All that Is, another term for everything, IS the infinitely creative consciousness that gives birth to your own infinitely creative consciousness. This Idea Construct is an excellent one to entertain when you are attempting to keep IN THE MOMENT. (humorously) I trust I have inspired you quite enough to be receptive to these subtle energies.

Perform your Ritual of Sanctuary

So I would suggest you relax. If you are sitting in a chair, make yourself comfortable. If you are lying down, prop up your upper body so that you will not fall asleep as you read this. Now imagine if you will, what I have defined as the Moment Point. Use your imagination and with your Inner Senses, imagine your current existence, the moment you are now experiencing, as somewhat more extended in duration than you have experienced moments in the past.

In Book Two, we provided an experiment for the reader to practice slowing down time within their Personal Reality Field. This is the same feeling we are creating here and now. You use your Intention to imbue your Moment Points with duration. Please make creative use of your Inner Senses to accomplish this, perhaps intuitively visualizing your present sensory images and sounds as slowing down, slowing down with your Intention.

What we are getting at here is a slowing down of time to the extent that we may glimpse the creation of physical objects from ideas. This would be Reality Construction viewed at the edge of creation. Now these are grand terms, and you might say I am making it all sound so easy, but at its heart, it IS the easiest thing in the world. You are experts at creating "something from nothing," and you can easily slow down this creative process to the microsecond level. Here you may see and feel what is involved in your creation of your Personal Reality Field. This includes your body and the senses you use to sense this manifestation activity.

How much must you slow down the act of reality creation to witness this? You will know you are meeting with success when you have a sensation of pulsing visually and as a felt sensation. This is the pulse of manifestation. This is the flow of the Subconscious Manifestation Energy Stream through the Coordinate Points and "into" the Reality Constructs.

(Seth is currently giving me a taste of this perspective. I am experiencing the pulsation. It feels like the heartbeat, only accelerated many times. Visually there is a dreamy quality. Briefly I experienced a twinge of fear, as if I was receiving forbidden knowledge. Possible religious programming? mf)

The flow of information "through" the Coordinate Point is so rich in imagery and other content that the researcher must intentionally slow down the flow of CUs through this gateway if they are to observe and study the construct.

Now can you imagine these theorized Coordinate Points as permeating "physical" space and matter, yet not taking up <u>any</u> space whatsoever? Let us refer to the CPs as etheric in nature in this experiment. They are the nonphysical "precursors" of the "future" created Reality Constructs. They exist interdimensionally and holographically. They are each everywhere literally all of the time, past, present and future. They exist as the determinant "values" in the manifestation phenomenon. And again, consciousness in the form of CUs expresses intentionally, as in our experiments, or unintentionally, as in the unconscious co-creation of the human or elemental expressions of all the other varied forms of "substance" in your dimension. When you have received adequate information from your experiment, gradually disengage from the Trance State. Return to full sensory awareness.

Findings - Document your observations of the Reality Creation phenomenon.

CHAPTER FOUR

The Visionary

Dialogue - Radio Interview
8/3/06 1:36 PM

Mark: Any comments on the radio interview?
Seth: Yes Mark. In all, I felt that the interview went quite well. I transmitted the information the listeners required to understand this new work and to go on with the evolution of their Souls. The Holographic Insert was real. Our host received it and commented quite adequately on how she perceived it. Others perceived their encounters with the Insert. You will receive some added attention for this interview and it does indeed signify a quickened pace of development for our business. Now for some dictation, though it shall be brief, hopefully. (humorously)

The Visionary State

The visionary within your modern culture is a much maligned figure. This may be because you have come so far from your tribal communities, as "progress" takes you away from core experiences of community and shared spirituality. In the U.S.A. in particular, and most of your developed nations, you take great care to marginalize your visionaries, particularly when they begin to speak of radical transformations to come in your world. Here however, in our growing community, we honor the visionary and we accept the visionary state of consciousness as natural, normal and quite essential to the evolution of the human Soul and the human species.

The visionary has visions, quite simply, and these visions are experienced through the use of the intuitive faculties. The visions of these seers of society are filled with Light. The visionary is enlightened, you see, and senses the foundation of reality as the Light Energy that it indeed is. In our view, we see all of humanity as potential visionaries.

Who is Responding?

Where does this visionary energy perspective originate? Let me explain with reference to the "typical" reader of my works. A moment... You have, Dear Reader, I am sure, what you refer to as your personal resources of wit, humor, creativity. This is that aspect of your psyche that you rely on to "come through" with the appropriate responses in your dealings with your world. Another way to describe this might be that these spontaneous responses that you give when required, these are the material of the free-flow of your conscious state. You seem to be accessing your personal reservoir of experience from which you create "answers" to the challenges of your environment, whether these challenges are human beings or circumstances that challenge you to feed back with appropriate germane information, behaviors, and so on. Now my questions to you would be, "Who is responding with this information? Who is the witty, the humorous, the creative one?"

Beings of Light

Let me answer my own questions. Beings of Light are responding. You ARE a Being of Light. You are a Soul with a body. You are a multitude of personalities existing in many different eras on your Earth, on other planets and in probable systems. You are experiencing your amnesia in the Third Dimension, perhaps scoffing at this admittedly "far out" narrative, yet it remains quite true that YOU are what we are talking about when we describe the Beings of Light. EVERYTHING in physical reality is "lighted" by Beings of Light, Gestalts of Consciousness, Light Bodies, Energy Bodies. They are the energy and incipient matter templates for all forms in physical reality and all other dimensions. So that any discussions as to whether Beings of Light exist are really quite humorous, as these Gestalts of Consciousness comprise ALL of human experience.

Perhaps what we are truly saying here, is that you are an Etheric Being. The witty, the humorous and the creative responses are from the nonphysical personality aspects that form your Soul Self. This is your true identity then. You are grounded in the nonphysical world.

Identity and the Shift

Now you become what you think about. Your identity is created from the ideas and images that you entertain within your mental environment, including messages sent to you from your Simultaneous Lives. Your identity is quite fluid. You are continuously assessing your mental, physical and emotional spheres of activity and assembling your identity from data gathered in this investigation.

You have many colleagues in this endeavor - the reassessment of the Personal and Consensus Realities. Your modern world in this timeframe is witnessing the transformation of the human mentality on a grand scale. Your fellow inhabitants of your planet are questioning their roles and duties as human beings and many are acknowledging the TRUTH of this matter of identity.

For example: many who have been skeptics are engaged in a reversal of thinking. They are "seeing the light" quite literally in all of their experiences, particularly where they have sought to keep the truth from their fellow humans. These transformations will be shocking to some, for they occur so abruptly that the breath is taken away. Yet as this event in the lives of men and women becomes more commonplace, the basic correctness and obvious necessity of this wholesale change in human perception and attitude will be recognized. The visionary of old is reborn in the present, during this shift - the Fourth-Dimensional Shift we are describing to you in our new books.

The Visionary of Old

The Personal Reality of the visionary of old may shed some light on this discussion. Now the demeanor of the visionary was one of complete absorption with the forces of nature. However, this was not a pass-time activity. This immersion in the natural elements - to the degree that the participant would experience their existence as an integral part of the world - was their normal waking experience.

You might say that the visionary was attending to spiritual matters on a moment-to-moment basis. They were, quite literally, in constant contact with their Guides, the Energy Personality and others, as well as the many Gestalts of Consciousness that represent the energetic supports of your systems on Earth. There are indeed Nature Spirits, for example, that may be contacted and with whom relationships may be cultivated by human beings. ALL of your Earthly reality is supported by spirit in various stages of complexity.

The visionary, then, was quite often enthralled with the experiencing of visions of various types, transmitted from their "pantheon" of sacred energy bodies into their opened or awakened consciousness.

Holographic Inserts

The preferred method of communication between the complex Gestalts of Consciousness you know as spirits, Guides, Angels and such, and the student in physical reality - the visionary - has always been the Holographic Insert. This is our name for a brief multisensory experience that is transmitted from the nonphysical being to the student. It is quite brief, usually, merely a fraction of a second in duration. It has Loving energy attached to it so that you will remember it. These are the visions that are experienced by students through the ages and documented in sacred texts of various kinds.

The visionary experience is really a conversation between the nonphysical beings and the student. It is not necessarily a one-way conversation. The Nature Spirit, for example, does not transmit communication streams into the consciousness of an unprepared student. The student most probably has first been prepared through study and through continued communications and Lessons created by the Spirit for the further education of the student. The student asks for the communication and the Spirit complies when appropriate.

Now, Holographic Inserts "pour off the page" for you, when you take the care to accept these multisensory messages within your mental awareness. These words and these phrases have power when they are considered carefully with the expectation of the manifested reality to be indeed made manifest.

It is an openness, really, a state of courageous expectation that you must cultivate. It is the same with spiritual literature of all types. The words do have power. The phrases, when they are considered after the required preparation of the human mentality, may initiate the unfolding of the Higher Consciousness. We may also relate this to all types of inspirational literature. It calls to you for specific reasons, to catalyze within you - the individual human - the resources required for the exploration of your inner world.

Inspirational Texts

For your information, Dear Reader, the ideas and philosophies of the great leaders of your perceived past are available to you within the milieu of your personal consciousness. Now obviously, this is the psychic mechanism for the inspiration and motivation of vast numbers of devotees to follow the great religious leaders, for example. It is a psychic network, a Telepathic Network that one participates in to make these connections. The catalyst for such a voyage of discovery or quest for understanding and knowledge, could be as simple as the reading of a book authored by one of these respected leaders.

As I related to you in my Second Book, the printed words within your spiritual and philosophical texts have power on the subtle levels. In a sense, these words serve to "open doors" within the psyche of the reader to allow for the reception of Divine Knowledge. This stream of energy has its source or transmission point within the after-death consciousness or Soul Self of the deceased writer.

So the selection of inspirational texts is very important in this project. You may find that certain authors "call out" to you in some way. You are drawn to particular authors, just as you may have been drawn to my works. It is a very natural thing to act upon these inspirational impulses. These mental constructs, the motivating impulses, serve as markers along the way, as you make your voyage of self discovery, the discovery of your Soul Self.

Now the questions may arise, "What is my relationship to these authors? Why do I feel compelled to seek out their books and read them?" The answers are that you are connected to a virtually limitless "family" of incarnated and currently "deceased," in your terms, human Souls. These are your Simultaneous Lives, that I described in my first two books. These are your etheric Guides also, your Energy Personality and other assistants, and these are the authors of inspirational texts.

Resonance

When you state, for example, that something "resonates" with you, this is a statement of literal fact. Let us say that you are speaking of some particularly evocative material you are reading in a book. You find yourself becoming quite affected by the ideas in the text. You become emotionally invested in the material. It seems as though the author is "reading your mind," as to what you are thinking and feeling. This vibratory resonance occurs when the thoughts you are entertaining within your consciousness are vibrating at a similar rate as the ideas you are reading about in the book. In this instance, the Consciousness Units that compose the thoughts held in the mental environment are vibrating at the same frequency as the ideas, images and other material elicited by the written words.

(On reading this after the dictation, Seth decided to imme-diately add the following three paragraphs. mf)

Now in this activity of resonance, you might say that the energetic potential of the one, assists in creating the holographic replicant within the other. This is a rather simplified way of expressing the manifestation phenomenon, in that the one "brings the other up" to a station of equally evolving manifestation - streamlining, energizing and facilitating the assemblage of the CUs within the other.

Now the reverse is also true here. It is a mutual sharing of energies in this resonance. There is a form of homeostasis or balance that is achieved once the level of Value Fulfillment is reached that is the "goal," in a sense, of the Reality Creation project. These discussions may become quite etheric. However, in its simplest form we may say that your reality is co-created from the Consciousness Units that are charged with the life force of All That Is.

The resonance phenomenon exists as a cohesive force in the assemblage of Consciousness Units into Reality Constructs throughout your Third-Dimensional Reality. When we speak in the new material of the researcher "fine tuning" the Inner Senses, we are saying that the researcher may achieve a similarity of vibratory frequency within their mental environment to the Reality Constructs that they wish to manifest. When this similarity of vibratory frequency is created - through our various techniques, for example - resonance is achieved. The Consciousness Units within your mental sphere resonate with their holographic counterparts - the "generic atoms" we have spoken of earlier. What is imagined on the "inner" is made manifest on the "outer" in this way.

This cohesive force is the electromagnetic energy we have mentioned that is at the basis of all created realities. The bioelectric energy that "lights and powers" the human body construct or any living or inanimate object, does so in a resonating, flashing on-and-off fashion. Here again we are referencing my past discussions with you on the nature of the atoms or Consciousness Units as they create multidimensional realities, in a sense, flashing or vibrating at specific rates to create the realities that vibrate at that particular frequency. You may also remember our discussion from our second book in which we presented the possibility for the researcher to experiment with modulating the frequency of their physical body construct to create healing.

Teaching Aids of the Nonphysical Beings

I do not wish to repeat myself too greatly in this new material, but allow me to once again state the ultimate premise of your Third-Dimensional existence. Your world is composed of Light. Each and every Reality Construct is the "visible" manifestation of Gestalts of Consciousness of various types.

The leaf on the tree before you is the "outward" creation of the "inner" thoughtform or Energy Gestalt of LEAF. The Beings of Light, therefore, exist at all levels of physical Reality Creation. And again, each and every Gestalt of Consciousness, including the Beings of Light, may be contacted through the Rituals of Contact and Communication we are presenting in these new works. In this way, the researcher may communicate with the leaf in question through an attunement of the vibratory frequency of the researcher's mental environment to the frequency of the subject i.e. LEAF.

Jung

In other models, these primal blueprints are referred to as "archetypes." Your eminent psychiatrist and researcher Jung popularized this term, as elemental to his theory of consciousness. Naturally this theory of Jung's bears a resemblance to the ideas within this current work. Jung was informed by The Seth Entity. He was first informed through contact and communication with his Energy Personality, and later used this Energy Construct as a bridge to the greater Gestalt of Consciousness to which he was associated - The Seth Entity, broadly speaking. Essentially, this was the path used by all three of the <u>recognized</u> Seth book authors in your timeframe. It is also the recommended path for those of you who wish to receive energy from the greater Energy Construct of which you are a part, be that The Seth Entity or any others.

Visionary Leaders

We suggested in our last book that there are true visionaries among you who are making themselves known. These are the advocates for your Mother Earth, the speakers, the teachers, the magicians, shamans, witches and healers of your timeframe, who are exerting considerable pressure on the current ruling regime - I am speaking in global terms here now - to "soften" and indeed spiritualize their expressions in physical reality, including their political systems. They are now coming forward to lead you in all the domains of human interaction.

Your leaders who have taken advantage of the people are now finding themselves "uncovered" and suddenly vulnerable. In their place there is becoming apparent this new class of "natural born leaders." We have stated that these visionaries will not necessarily be elected. They lead in a very appropriate manner, for that is their natural gift, as humans in this very important era in your world.

Perhaps now you have witnessed this phenomenon, essentially a calling forth to those of goodwill from your Mother Earth, to tend to THE TRUE BUSINESS AT HAND. The denial is lifting, you see, as many of you begin to see the damage done by your leaders with your tacit approval.

Or perhaps you have experienced this phenomenon in a more personal way, as you may have felt yourself called to serve your fellow humans in a more direct way than you have done in the past. Leaders come in many forms. Leading by example, to coin a phrase, is a wholly adequate and necessary service one may provide to initiate the rebuilding of your damaged societies.

You see, there are no authorities among these visionary leaders. They do not hold power by virtue of authority, such as a power "over" others. They are powerful because they keep their own power. They do not give up their authority to others. In the broad sense, ALL of you are becoming enlightened, empowered with the natural creative energies that are your birthright. You are all becoming leaders in this way.

Mystery Civilizations

As descendants of the divine rulers of the Mystery Civilizations, the visionary leaders are engaged in the same sort of activities as their predecessors. They are part of a lineage of incarnation in your Third Dimension. Now genetically, there may or may not be a connection, however the Soul Family connections are there to investigate.

For example: those of you who have identified an Atlantean heritage, through our experimentation or other research efforts, may be interested to know that the leadership within the Atlantean culture itself was initially drawn from what you might call the "spiritual" class. This group fulfilled several different functions in the society. They were scientists of nonphysical reality, what we are calling the Scientist of Consciousness. These humans were raised from birth as the "magical child" we spoke of in the last book. They had memories of all of their Reincarnational Existences. This information, which included "future" experiences, was quite valuable. The leaders were visionaries in the true sense of that term, in that they were aware of the probable events to occur in the future of their societies.

Divine King

You may read about the "vestiges" of the class of prophet leaders in your stories of the Divine King. In successive civilizations after the "fall" of Atlantis, for example, this idea was kept alive, if only symbolically, in the concept of the King or Emperor having a direct connection to the Divine. You may also read in your histories how ultimately this type of leadership failed miserably, for the leaders took the power without taking the responsibility of divine leadership. They were more interested in ruling than leading. In your current leadership on your Earth, you may see this ultimate act of hubris in the leaders who have anointed themselves as the modern Divine King, yet choose to deny the citizenry their rights, and as I said, rule rather than lead.

Ancient Engineers

There was another serving class, another group of humans within the Atlantean society, that was dedicated to assisting the people within their social group in terms of leadership and the creation of social and political structures as well as <u>physical</u> structures. This group was composed of humans who were extremely talented in the mathematical sciences and had a natural affinity for numbers, figures and their manipulation. They were natural engineers and experts at what you might call the "hard sciences." These humans "instinctively" knew the most efficient methods for creating a structure, such as a house or other building, and possessed a facility for designing and building dams and other large structures.

These ancient engineers were also visionaries, just as the visionary leaders were prophets as well as gifted politicians. They could foretell the future stresses - from natural disasters etc. - that a particular structure of their design would incur after being built, and so could design and build the structure with this prophetic material in mind.

Time Machine

The engineers were not limited to design and creation of buildings and other structures. They were instrumental in the creation of vehicles that were used by researchers to "travel" interdimensionally. I am now transmitting a Holographic Insert into Mark's mental field in an attempt to graphically illustrate one of the interdimensional vehicles.

(I received the transmission. I could see an image of a crystalline structure, egg-shaped, and within it sat the researcher. The material seemed to be some sort of "spun" substance, yet faceted, darkish gray in color. The vehicle resembled a "buckyball" or some other geodesic form. mf)

Now these vehicles did not "travel" in the common meaning of that term. The crystal structure assisted the researcher in an attunement of their consciousness through vibratory resonance. The mental Intention of the researcher, directed through the "focal" aspects of the crystal structure, allowed for the "bringing in" of the Simultaneous Lives lived in different points in space and time. Interdimensional travel is always about time travel in your system. The future, in your terms, is really just your progressed reality in linear time. Your future is another dimension, a dimension that exists, as I have stated, within the exact same CUs that compose you the reader, as well as all of the current Reality Constructs that compose your world.

Multidimensional CU Expression

To illustrate my last point: imagine if you will, your current existence in this day, within this moment that you are reading these words. Can you visualize how the book, with its CUs "holding" its shape through the Coordinate Points we have discussed, exists also as, let us say, a section of a tree in front of you in a life you may be living as a forest dweller many years before your so-called Christian Era? Likewise in this example, these exact same CUs, as they flash on and off, creating different realities within different timeframes, do indeed compose different Reality Constructs of varied types within these different eras. This is why I describe the future and past timeframes as simply dimensions.

All timeframes or Reincarnational Existences exist "right before your eyes." You may conceptualize this, if it helps you, as a layered effect, with the different existences and their constructs simultaneously created "one on top of the other." I hope this description of the very easily accessible dimensions assists you in attempting contact with these other lives.

The lives are out there in front of you. They are perceived through the fine-tuning of the Inner Senses. This process is quite doable for the student of this material. Now for some experimentation.

Experiment - Precepts and Resonance
Hypothesis: by focusing on the precept you may catalyze the holographic insert from the entity.

You may with some preparation, feel the ecstasy and empowerment that comes with the experiencing of the Holographic Inserts I stream into my Third Subject's consciousness. I send them to Mark for purposes of elucidation and bringing Light and information to the discussion. I also present these "teaching aids" to you for the same purposes.

There are a few ways you may explain this to yourself - convince yourself that this phenomenon is real - so that you may indeed experience it clearly, without resorting to denial, fear, anxiety. The simplest explanation is that you are my student and as such you and I have a special, spiritual relationship. The connection here is a physical one also, relating to certain portals or chakras as you might call them, located on and around the physical body.

Any one of my precepts may be used as a Holographic Insert. We have mentioned before that the phrase "you create your own reality" is a particularly potent precept and stands as the foundational statement, if you will, of my entire Teaching. I would suggest an experiment to determine the precepts *(pages 36 & 37. mf)* that have the greatest "effects" for you, when you activate them as Holographic Inserts by focusing on them in your meditations.

Perform your Ritual of Sanctuary

Relax and enter a light Trance State. First, I would have you read the precepts and attempt to identify those that "speak" to you with the most energy and frequency. The phenomenon known as resonance comes into play here. Your physical construct, your human body, is actually a vibrating system of Consciousness Units, as you know. Ideas and images of all types, either entertained from within your mental environment or considered from written texts and other media, also "hold" their individual vibratory signatures.

Let me again emphasize that it is the Divine Essence cultivated within the student that is the catalyst here. Through working on yourself, through reading spiritual literature and engaging in these arcane practices, the researcher cultivates a certain perspective that allows for the experiencing of the Holographic Insert by the Inner Senses. Also, on "the other side," in a sense, the creator of the manuscript - in this case The Seth Entity - empowers the text with the essential energies of the Divine - All That Is - so that on the subtle levels where these types of spiritual growth and extra sensory and emotional perception are experienced, the stage is set quite well for the Holographic Inserts to display.

Now focus on your selected precepts one at a time. Have an Intention to link up with the etheric component of each precept. There is an openness required in this endeavor. You might think of yourself as an antenna in search of a signal here. Be quiet. Be still. Listen with your Inner Senses for the response from the Entity. **Findings** - Document your Findings in catalyzing the precepts into Holographic Inserts.

Experiment - Identifying Communication Streams within your Mental Environment
Hypothesis: in trance you may identify the communication streams within your mental environment.

Now we shall investigate the many information streams that "flow" through your cognitive awareness at any one time. The descriptive terms "flow" and "time" are used to hopefully facilitate your connecting to the data streams and to identifying and understanding the content. You are familiar with a flowing river. The river flows regardless of your noticing it, observing it, studying it. In a similar fashion, the many information streams that flow through your mental environment, do so regardless of your attention to them, your noticing them. However, though you may be unaware of these streams of divine information, and of course others that are most certainly not divine, you are indeed quite affected by the ideas and images carried within these many streams of communication. Here I believe it would be a good idea for the student to become more aware of the content of these information streams.

Perform your Ritual of Sanctuary

Relax and enter your Trance State, as usual. Now to begin, let us list the many providers of information that exist within the mind or psyche of the "typical" human engaged in co-creating an existence on your world.

First and foremost would be the divine source - All That Is. This data stream is quite easily recognized by the seeker of wisdom. The ecstasy felt during the encounter with the Divine, is the energy signature that marks this source.

Next on the list would be the "voices" of Soul Family members past, present and future.

Of course the Negative Entities are continually there, drawing upon your personal energy to feed their own Gestalts of Consciousness.

The self-created gods and goddesses exist there also, as well as the Energy Bodies of divine beings of various types created through the collective efforts of humanity over the ages.

Your own understanding of God with a capital G exists here as an energy form.

If you have pursued contact with the Elemental Beings, they exist within your mentality also, to the degree that you have co-created them through study, worship, observation, and so on.

Your Simultaneous Lives are there in their totality, providing information and both support and negative influence, according to what you are on your Earth to learn at this time.

Let us not forget your own ego/intellect that over-sees this phenomenon and indeed censors and directs the activities therein.

Now there are certainly more examples of Light Bodies and other Energy Forms that exist within your consciousness. Note these as you discover their activity in your experimentation. When you feel as though you have received enough information from this experiment, return to full sensory awareness.

Findings - Document your Findings in identifying the streams of information within your mental environment.

CHAPTER FIVE

Creating Positive Realities

Dialogue - Asking for What You Want
6/27/06 2:52 PM

Mark: Thanks for the continuing collaboration Seth.
Seth: You are quite welcome Mark. And as for the financial concerns you may be focused on currently, keep a Good Humor thought, my friend. All will be well. You are merely learning how to ask for what you want and need. You will get good at it over time.

Good Humor

You have perhaps noticed how Mark and I use humor quite liberally throughout our new books. There is an important reason for this: we are attempting to demonstrate to you the reader, the importance of the creation of simple Good Humor within your Reality Creation agendas. This aspect of consciousness serves as the basis for the Love Light that we covered in a previous chapter, in that the Good Humor precedes or "paves the way" for the establishment of the creative endeavor.

So Love Light is born in a simple Good Humor. I trust that this will not be a difficult stretch of the imagination for you to comprehend and accept this information. It is true that in your world, Good Humor may be thought of as a simple and mundane aspect of existence. It may be thought of as too trivial to be considered in as serious an endeavor as the creation of realities. Yet I am suggesting here that Good Humor is the starting point for the creation of realities, in particular, the positive realities that are the focus of this book.

Emotional Investment

You are literally born out of the Love AND Good Humor of All That Is. Here I am asking you to move beyond any religious conditioning that has convinced you that you perhaps were born out of suffering to live a life of pain. For in truth, the facts in this matter are just the opposite.

Let me state the obvious here, however, to avoid any misunderstanding. (humorously) Yes, your reality is born in your imagination out of Love and Good Humor, yet you will of necessity also experience the opposites of these attributes - fear, anxiety, anger, hatred. Now the important thing here, is how long you hold on to the fear, anxiety, anger and hatred. How much importance do you attach to these emotional states as you experience them? How much do you invest your ego/intellect in the recreation of these states, once you have allowed them to enter your mental environment?

Fear and Humor

Fear may be thought of as the founding energy in the emotional states of anxiety, anger and hatred. Now fear and Good Humor do not mix well. If one is enjoying the state of consciousness known as Good Humor, one is most probably enjoying THE ABSENCE OF FEAR. I stress the importance of Good Humor here for the simple reason that, because it is often so simple to generate this mental state, it becomes a very useful tool in the creation of Courage out of fear. Let me illustrate with an example, if I may.

Some of my students, upon reading my second book, have expressed the criticism that my experiments and exercises are quite challenging. To these students I say, simplify this endeavor. Bring this back to the basics of manifestation. Prepare your mental environment for the creation of positive realities by FIRST embodying or generating within your consciousness, the state of simple enjoyment or Good Humor.

Example - Using Good Humor

Now for the example... let us say that you are currently experiencing fear in its most basic form, perhaps dreading something that is to occur in your future, or perhaps fearing what has already occurred, perhaps fearing that the dreaded subject or object will continue to exist in your reality. As I have stated in my last two books, if you are experiencing fear, you are under the influence of Negative Entities - Energy Bodies that thrive on the emotions of fear and anxiety.

So perhaps a simple antidote to these energies would be for you to trivialize and make fun of these influences. By creating a state of simple Good Humor in your consciousness in this way, you are creating a comedy out of a fearful drama.

In the transformation, you are also creating Courage out of fear. Without getting into details, we could say that the natural abilities of human consciousness create this transformation of fear into Courage. You are, from the inception into a human body on Earth, created out of Love. Your consciousness may easily return to this positive state, then, with merely the least amount of effort on your part.

This is easy to do. Making fun of the fear-producing ideas or images may be an enjoyable and creative act unto itself. You are using your imagination to turn down the fearful intensity of the ideas and images, and perhaps replacing them with humorous images and ideas.

Do you see how you are much better prepared to create positive realities when you are in this self-created state of Good Humor? Certainly it is important to continue creating this positive state as you attempt to create a positive reality. It is the extension of the current moment of Good Humor into the future that creates the positive future.

So let us assume that you have gained some mastery over this creation of Good Humor within your own apparatus. You may notice that, over time, as you get good at creating Good Humor, the quality of your daily existence improves. This is the creation of positive realities in itself, as even modest improvements in an otherwise fearful and anxious

Reality Construction may have profound effects on your daily life. You create your world from the beliefs you hold about what is possible. As you embody the state of Good Humor consistently, it becomes possible for you to believe in the continuation of this positive state.

The Time is Now

Dear Reader, now in this moment of Good Humor resides your opportunity for an improved future. Perhaps a brief recap is in order here, to serve as a basis for this proclamation. (humorously) You create BOTH your past and your future from your current moment. This is one of the basic tenets of my Teaching, and so it would serve you well to use this fact of life as a "given" - an essential building block upon which rests my theoretical construct of Reality Creation. So when I suggest to you that you may expand your consciousness intentionally, perhaps what I really mean is that you are capable, simply by virtue of your existence on your physical Earth at this time, of truly exploring and embodying the richness of your momentary existence.

Yes, your life is a series of moments. In this series of moments, obviously, you are reading from my book. Now the act of reading requires some focus "in the moment." You must muster all of your attention and direct it toward the task of reading and absorbing the material. In a similar way, the student of my Teaching would do well to harness the same efforts of concentration entailed in the reading of this book, toward the appreciation and assessment of the current Moment Point - the spacious moment that connects all of your Simultaneous Lives.

Any moment will do here. This one... Or this one... Or this one... The study and appreciation of the spacious moment does indeed take some preparation. You are, in a sense, preparing yourself for the PROBABILITY of experiencing the moment of awakening - the moment of healing, the moment of perceiving the Abundant Universe, the moment of receiving Divine Wisdom. I am aware that in other Teachings, the student is taught that the awakening of the consciousness to its own spiritual heritage is a lifetime "undertaking," if you will excuse my pun. Here however, we are offering the student the opportunity to awaken without first expiring. (humorously)

Health and Holograms

Health - physical, mental, emotional, financial - is a state of consciousness that exists in a Moment Point in your perceptual reality. "Behind" this "spiritual" assessment is your Soul Self, the co-creator with All That Is of your Personal Reality Field.

Mark, I just sent you a brief hologram demonstrating how all of the subatomic elements of awarized energy that comprise your Third-Dimensional world for you personally, collaborate to create this awareness of health. *(The hologram lasted less than a second. I was suddenly quite knowledgeable about the intricacies of how each Consciousness Unit in my perceptual field validates my beliefs and expectations in the moment. It was a very pleasant moment. Ecstatic and empowering and reassuring. mf)*

Now speaking of physical health: this is the reason that your world and everything in it seems to support your physical symptoms, you see. Your field of Personal Reality creation, because it is a reflection, a direct reflection of your inner world, does continuously reflect your personal symptoms that you are experiencing/creating for purposes of learning and Value Fulfillment. The improvements desired in your physical health, therefore, must obviously come from a change in this inner perception. We have been referring to these inner perceptive processes as the Inner Senses. We will go much deeper into this method in The Healing Regimen.

Experiment - Moments of Awakening
Hypothesis: your sleeptime activities may assist in your spiritual awakening.

You do have many awakenings in your day-to-day existence, and these can be opportunities for accessing the spiritual awakening we seek. For example: each time you awaken from sleep, you have an opportunity to awaken also in a spiritual sense. As I have described to you in these new manuscripts, your nighttime activities entail a great deal of what you might term "spiritual" or "Soul-directed" activities. Yet on your awakening after sleep, the rigors of physical existence usually demand that you forget about these nocturnal adventures. Before you go to sleep...

Perform your Ritual of Sanctuary

You will carry your state of Sanctuary into the dreamstate. Then take a few moments as you awaken from your sleep times to consider what you may have experienced in the previous hours or minutes. I would suggest that you go beyond the usual documentation of dream content and pursue an analysis of the broad indicators that may point the way to the learning of your primary and secondary Lessons.

This would mean that you would certainly continue to document your dream activities, as I have suggested to you in the second book, yet you may go a step further in this discovery process by "guessing" or "imagining" what might be the broader concepts and ideas illustrated by the dream content. You might try to briefly - in a short sentence - describe the sleep-time activities as a whole. Here you are working on the premise that your sleeptime activities have meaning for you personally. It is my suggestion that these activities hold the key to your understanding of your purpose on Earth.

I believe it would be adequate for you to spend perhaps only a very few minutes in this analysis of your nighttime activities. Upon awakening you are already in a relaxed and contemplative state of consciousness. Merely suggest to yourself upon awakening that you can summarize the preceding activities and Lessons in a short sentence. Allow yourself to create this sentence for a few moments and then document it in the medium of your choice. After several days of this documentation you may well see patterns emerge in your Findings.

Findings - Document in your journal or other medium your Findings from this ongoing experiment.

Prelude to the Regimens

The Lessons you are learning currently may be categorized according to the three broad topics we will cover in the next three chapters of this manuscript. This is a continuation of our discussion on the blessing "healthy, wealthy and wise" from our last book.

Now **health** would obviously entail Lessons learned regarding the physical body, mind and spirit. We are asserting here that the symptoms and illnesses humans generate within their bodies are for educational purposes. Each illness is a physical expression of inherently nonphysical Idea Constructs.

The same may be said of **prosperity**. The Lessons of the acquisition of wealth and the utilization of that form of energy is spiritual at its base. Money and wealth are simply very potent ideas pertaining to security and value in the physical domain. So here again, the physical is simply the observable component of the invisible, nonphysical spiritual construct.

The **wisdom** of the Soul, the third element in this blessing, may be accomplished in the learning of these symbolic Lessons in physical reality by allowing these life Lessons to transform the psyche. Loving Understanding and Courage are some of the results of this transformative phenomenon.

Let us now explore these Lessons in detail.

CHAPTER SIX

The Healing Regimen

Dialogue - Physical Challenges
6/14/06 10:43 AM

Seth: *Mark I am well aware of your physical challenges and how they impact our work together. Your thought that you would prefer I not continue to give you the "cheerleader" updates is well taken. Remember here that these prophecies are based on the most probable outcomes if you were to follow on your current trajectory. Thus, if you are currently in a positive frame of mind, the probabilities for a positive future are quite good. Now, if you slip into a less than positive frame of mind, the probabilities for a positive future are greatly diminished. Do you follow me?*

Mark *Yes Seth. It's pretty basic. I forget how basic it is.*

Seth: *My advice to you Mark is the same as it has always been. Create your positive future NOW with your positive life-affirming beliefs and ideas.*

Gestalts of Consciousness and Health

Let us review the basics for purposes of creating The Healing Regimen. As you well know, you are a Soul within a physical body and with All That Is you co-create your existence in Third-Dimensional Reality. In this endeavor you cooperate with each and every Consciousness Unit in your perceptive field. The "blueprints" for your creative works are the beliefs, thoughts and images that predominate in your mental environment. These blueprints exist as arrays of Coordinate Points within the pre-manifestation domains. These arrays merge to create Gestalts of Consciousness - complex affiliations of mental constructs - that are, in essence, the nonphysical representations of EVERYTHING.

Thus, ideas and images relative to a concept identified as "the common cold," for example, assemble into Gestalts of Consciousness, representing the accumulated "wisdom," you might say, from all human experience of the common cold. All of the "requirements" for achieving the common cold are present. The symptoms are there within these incipient Reality Constructs. In a sense, you could say that the operating system for the cold virus is "resident" within these mental constructs. The symptoms exist in potentiality. They await the invocation of the disease state into the mental environment of the human.

Now, the "disease process," as you call it, exists first as a mental vulnerability. This is not the accepted view, I certainly realize. However, bear with me for just a moment and

I believe you may receive useful information... the mental precedes the physical in all matters of disease process. But of course, there must be the physical "cause" of the illness. The mental and thus the emotional vulnerability creates a physical vulnerability through suggestion. "I am near those who have colds, I will get a cold," "I am old and vulnerable to disease, I will get a cold." The continual presentation to the inner mental environment that you are vulnerable - either through your own internal ruminations or through the transmissions from other Energy Bodies - creates the physical vulnerability, such as a weakened immune system, so that exposure to a particular strain of virus would then "lead" to the creation of the disease state in the body and the "inevitable" progression of the illness through to its conclusion.

Perhaps I should elaborate on my statement that the suggestions "create" physical vulnerabilities within the body. These suggestions or thoughts or potent images, from whatever source, are the same as any other thoughts or images generated by consciousness, in that they seek manifestation within the physical and other dimensions.

In the case of disease process, we find that the creation of imbalance occurs on a cellular level. So that if you might envision a cell within the body as it exists within the organ or blood or perhaps muscle tissue as being subject to the messages of the various control centers of the body - the brain and the many systems that feed "information" to the cells to govern their activity, such as the immune, digestive

93

and other systems - do you see how the mental suggestions might serve to short-circuit some of these information streams?

A simple example here for illustration, would be the difficulties that may come from a sensitive person observing
distasteful images while they eat. They may incur a bad
case of indigestion from these mental suggestions from
their perceived environment. It is my suggestion that ALL
illnesses and their symptoms, are caused by these Gestalts
of Consciousness, in this case by an Energy Body you might
call Indigestion.

The Medical Model

As with all of your creations in physical reality, you could
say that you are entranced by your own projections, including the bodily states known as "symptoms and illnesses."
Now I have spoken in other manuscripts of the dangers in
your medical community of constantly referring to the "inevitability" of certain illnesses forming in the human body.
Statistics are bandied about SUGGESTING that such-and-
such a percentage of men or women will INEVITABLY
"fall victim" to certain diseases. Do you see where I am
taking this discussion? The disease process is supported
on the SUGGESTIONS of Gestalts of Consciousness.
And so you might say that the great majority of your medical doctors are "under the spell" of these Energy Bodies.
They are entranced with this Gestalt of Consciousness, the
central information center called the medical model. They

have been for many years indoctrinated with the data and procedures that support this system.

You play your part in this drama also, Dear Reader. It is your role to "pretend" that what the doctors say is true. You obediently create the applicable symptoms within your body. You are supporting your health practitioner in this way. "Doctor's orders" DEMAND that you create a particular set of symptoms to correspond to a particular disease state. This collaboration takes place on the subtle levels, of course. The telepathic communication streams are quite active between Gestalts of Consciousness of various types, the doctor and the patient. Everyone must do their part here in order to sustain the "appearance" of illness and the "appearance" of healing or perhaps failure to heal, initiated by the medical profession.

It is all supported on suggestion. These suggestions are essentially Idea Constructs that are the building blocks of disease and the treatment of disease. Thus you have, for example, a Gestalt of Consciousness known as Alzheimer's Disease. The patient dutifully exhibits all of the symptoms of that disease. The patient is experiencing this illness as a vehicle for the learning of particular Lessons. In the case of Alzheimer's, Lessons of infantilism and being cared for without protest, are often the reasons for the creation of the disease state, though it is not wise to generalize in these matters.

Ultimately however, illnesses of all kinds are created as life Lessons. The disease state is a teacher to you in physical reality. Your Soul Self, your Guides and all members of your Soul Family are engaged with you in the drama of physical illness. You are learning your Lessons as a collective, much as you would study and learn within a classroom in one of your universities.

Now to elaborate on this comparison here... just as you would learn in a classroom the subject matter in a course on, shall we say, Life Science, everything needed to pass that course, in The Healing Regimen you may discover the truths in the Lessons of physical existence. As you become knowledgeable on the causes of your malady, you may find the means to learn your Lesson in other ways, perhaps in ways that do not entail physical symptoms and disease. This is always your free will choice. You may decide to continue the Lesson of physical illness or you may decide to discover the "causes" and address them.

magician shaman witch healer

In The Healing Regimen, just as in other matters of intentional Reality Creation, the idea is to become cognizant of your unconscious agendas of manifestation IN THE MOMENT. In this moment of awakening, you may use your will to begin the creation of improved Reality Constructs with regards to your physical being, i.e. the transformation of symptoms and "disease states" to a lack of symptoms and the perception of "healed" body states.

Now our approach requires a definite change of perspective for the average reader. Please allow me to present some background to this discussion for those of you who may be new to this material. In my last book I encouraged you take on the roll of Scientist of Consciousness. And as a specialist in the use of the Inner Senses, I asked you to go about your investigations in this ongoing "altered state." I reminded you that the Scientist of Consciousness was the magician, the shaman, the witch of antiquity. You were simply affirming your connection to these original scientists from your perceived past. As you embodied the suggested role of Scientist of Consciousness, you "put on" the perceptual lenses of the witch or the shaman or the healer.

In this new project of ours, as you intentionally create this altered state within your mental environment, you will enable your Inner Senses to "pick up" the vibrational messages of Consciousness Units that exist within the nonphysical domains. These are the energy signatures of specific Gestalts of Consciousness, some representing, shall we say, "disease process," and others representing "healing process."

Both disease and healed states, as well as all states in between, exist in the moment. Your goal as researcher is to determine with your Inner Senses, the influences from the various Gestalts of Consciousness and how they assist in the creation of your particular malady or the malady of your subject. Then you shall use your Metaphorical Tools to diminish or eliminate these influences - guided by the Gestalts of Consciousness representing healing process - so that the body may return to balance.

Let us briefly discuss the related views of some of the indigenous peoples of your Earth. We often make these comparisons in our discussions to illustrate that the unknown reality is already quite well known to some of you. For example: in the spiritual traditions among the First People of your human race, an intimate relationship exists between the human and the environment. It is common to speak to Nature directly in these collectives and receive responses from trees, stones, animals etc. These humans are well aware of the consciousness and integrity of plants, animals and the various elements around them. They accept that a rock has a spirit, that fire has a spirit that may be addressed and that will respond.

Just as the indigenous peoples communicate with the spirits of the natural world, it is possible for you on The Healing Regimen to seek counsel from these Energy Forms, what we are calling Gestalts of Consciousness. You do this through the use of your Inner Senses, observing The Emotional Body.

The Emotional Body

The Emotional Body is the energy center of your human body within which the signatures of the various Energy Forms may be perceived. As we have stated in a previous chapter, within the electromagnetic corona it is the central plane, the focus of the intersecting energies that comprise the Light Body. This nonphysical construct may be visualized as an oval form of pulsating light energy suspended within the heart region of the physical body. Of course, you may sense it in your individual ways. This form is perceived with the Inner Sense of sight we have named Auric Vision.

In my theory, emotion is the great creative force within your system that serves to push the incipient Reality Constructs into physicality. We have described this in a very basic way in our last book and in preceding chapters in this manuscript. Let me summarize this material. It is ALL about emotion in your world. You exist within Third-Dimensional Reality. You create your world according to the various thoughts and images within your mental environment AND the templates for creation that exist as Gestalts of Consciousness. You cooperate with EVERYTHING IN YOUR EXISTENCE in this play of consciousness you are experiencing that you call "my life."

Now everything in created reality exists as a particular frequency or vibration of emotion, what we have referred to as "bioelectric energy." Everything is alive. Everything is composed of this Light Energy. You might think of these individual vibrations as the "emotional charge" that both creates and sustains the Reality Construct - whatever that might be - in time and space in your system.

This idiosyncratic vibrational signature, for example, is how I Seth may identify my subject Mark here, when we wish to communicate with one another. He has a specific frequency or emotional Energy Form that he displays, as do you all. These frequencies are perceived through the Inner Senses, so that you may "see" the frequency, "hear" the frequency and so on. These senses tend to blend together somewhat, as we have stated earlier.

Since all Energy Bodies have their own individual emotional charge or frequency, where there are issues of symptoms and illness, there are the attendant Energy Forms representing these constructs that are observable within The Emotional Body. Also within this Emotional Body there are observable Energy Constructs that will lead you to "solutions" - the healing and balance you are seeking. We might call these Gestalts of Consciousness the nonphysical "data banks" that hold the collected wisdom and experience of healing from the practices of magicians, shamans, witches and healers.

Another way to describe this repository of healing might be to briefly speak on the subject of "spontaneous healing," as you call it. Now your literature is filled with stories of humans who have "garnered their inner resources" to effect miraculous changes in their debilitating physical conditions. Of course, to the human raised within a society that stresses the medical model, these transformations from deathly ill to completely healed are indeed perceived as miraculous. Yet, if we view disease process and the medical model as Gestalts of Consciousness, may we also conceive of Spontaneous Healing as simply another readily accessible Gestalt of Consciousness? The Gestalt of Consciousness you might call Spontaneous Healing is the "transmitter" that you "tune-in" to with your Metaphorical Tools to receive the signal - the "stream of healing energy and information" - that you will use to create the necessary changes within the body for the transformation.

Healing Power of Love

Your emerging reality is composed of Light, as we have said. You might say that the Coordinate Points within the juncture of time and space of any particular Moment Point of your physical existence, serve to "hold the shape" of the emerging reality, the outgrowth, if you will, of the Subconscious Manifestation Energy Stream. This context for Reality Creation is indeed the Love Light Matrix. The atoms or Consciousness Units are each, again as we have suggested to you, energized, animated, empowered by Love with a capital L.

Your world is an ongoing manifestation created from the Loving energies of All That Is. All That Is *IS* Love, and so it follows that Reality Constructs of all types are founded in Love. Now within your Consensus Realities on Earth at this time, there is a pronounced diversion AWAY from Love. You may see this in all of your social, political and even your religious institutions.

It is obvious, is it not? Your world is in crisis. It is increasingly difficult to find Love in your reality. It is true that there is a Turnabout that is occurring, as you as a race are turning back to Love. But do you see how the absence of Love is so damaging to humanity? See it and remember it.

Now with regards to human health and healing, it is the same: wherever Love is absent, you will surely find decay, illness, disease, imbalance. I am not telling you something you do not already know here. Dear Reader, you are conceived in Love, but you are diverted by other emotions as you live your life. The consistent experiencing of the Negative Emotions results in the creation of symptoms and disease. Now in a sense, The Healing Regimen is a matter of peeling away the residue of Negative Emotion that hardens like a shell around The Emotional Body. Underneath this shell you will find the core of your humanity - Love, just as we have been describing.

These emotions of Love and Compassion serve a very important purpose here in this project. They are the forces the practitioner uses to effect healing and balance. So that here, in a very elementary way, Negative Emotions serve to create symptoms and disease, whereas Loving Understanding and compassion serve to create healing and balance. Again, emotion is an Electromagnetic Entity that serves as the impetus or natural energy source for the creation of Reality Constructs.

In this suggestion you may also see a strategy for approaching the Healing Quest you are to begin. Human emotion, directed in, shall we say, dramatic and even shocking ways, is the concentrated force that the co-creator employs to "push" into manifestation the desired reality of healing. So that success here is determined by the intensity of desire you can consistently muster within the Rituals of Healing we will cover momentarily.

Guides and Healing

What is the value, (in so much as these words may be valued by you,) of the messages of Beings of Light? Some would say, of course, that these messages are priceless. The words are, after all, the messages of spirits - those who no longer exist as physical beings, such as myself. If this is so, then should you worship these messages and these beings? Historically, humans have projected their own innate divinity onto these representations - god and goddess, spirit being etc. Yet at the same time, the human devalues their own contribution. The human projects the god within onto an outside entity, and then slavishly worships it, forgetting the origins of the god from within the human psyche.

We are discussing these matters in an attempt to remind you the reader of your innate divinity. You are a god. You are a goddess. This is a fact of life. As you begin to accept this condition, perhaps you will also remember that you have the power to heal yourself and others.

Now as with all healing activities from your perceived past - within shamanic cultures for example - you will have help in The Healing Regimen. You will have assistance from your Guides. Your Guides are emissaries from All That Is - the source of all realities, the Loving center of the created Universes.

So it is quite naturally that you turn to your Guides to assist in The Healing Regimen. Your Guides know what Love is and can remind you of this over the course of the project. Your Guides, such as the Energy Personality and others, may facilitate the healings that take place within the physical body. They help you to maintain the required intensity of emotion over the long term.

In my book on Soul Evolution, I offered the reader an experiment designed to explore the use of the Energy Personality to best advantage. I suggested that the reader think of this Guide as a personal assistant, one that would be "on call" to assist in matters of importance, such as the learning of Lessons. The Energy Personality may serve as a divine assistant for you in this project. At the end of this chapter we shall offer an experiment in which you may call in your Guides for help on this Healing Quest. For now, let us discuss the Light Body and the means to explore it with the Inner Sense of sight.

Auric Vision and Healing

You might say that what your New Age healers refer to as the human Aura, is essentially your "timeless" Light Body. The Aura is a reflection of your greater Soul Self THROUGH the Consciousness Units that compose your current physical body. Now within this you may detect, by using what we are calling your Auric Vision, the exhibits of electromagnetic emanations of Gestalts of Consciousness of all types. Within this Auric Vision you could, as a Scientist of Consciousness, diagnose past, present and future life issues. All of your many Simultaneous Lives exhibit their activities in an essential form within this Aura.

Each Consciousness Unit "remembers" each and every one of its voyages into form. These Consciousness Units tell their stories, and if you listen carefully, you may discover the proper path to take to heal and balance the human subject - yourself, a friend or family member or possibly even a leader who has gone astray and requires an "adjustment" on the Etheric Plane. (humorously)

Here, with an understanding of the animate Universe we are describing in these new books, it becomes quite possible for the Scientist of Consciousness to assume the role of Healer, and in a manner of speaking, "address" the Gestalts of Consciousness that support the malady. Thus the healer is "speaking" to the disease and acting on the responses to effect the healing.

Now when you use your Auric Vision, the information comes to you in unique ways, in a fashion distinct from your normal Third-Dimensional perceptions. Your Auric Vision may present you with a literal dramatization of the issues and problems inherent in the malady you are observing. This Inner Sense may project onto your inner field of perception, perhaps as you close your eyes, complete scenes peopled with characters of various descriptions. These dramatizations of the malady and the cure may run the gamut from literal representations to those that are so deeply personal and symbolic that only YOU would know the meanings entailed.

For example: you might view a scene in which a human heart is literally "broken." And let us further state that the destroyer of the heart is a person easily recognized as your relative or friend or lover. Do you see the literal representation here? It is trying to tell you something. Most of you would probably interpret this scene in similar ways.

Or in another example: suppose that you viewed a scene that contained a surreal display of images accompanied by a changing stream of emotion. In this case, you are called upon to consult your personal symbols, utilizing images, ideas and emotions that only YOU would understand, to interpret the material. Your interpretation and your diagnosis style will be a direct reflection of your personality aspects. You will diagnose and treat in your preferred fashion, using what works best for you.

Divine Will

As you co-create your Personal Reality Field, you might say that All That Is "supplies" the energy for your creations in the form of Consciousness Units infused with Love. This infusion occurs within a context of the Love Light Matrix. We have discussed this metaphor in earlier chapters. Let me present a synopsis here for you. ALL realities created by consciousness are based in Love. Yet in Third-Dimensional Reality there exists the OPPOSITE of Love that serves as a counterpoint and is quite necessary within your linear time illusion. The counterpoint to Love, what we might call Negative Emotion, serves to create alternatives in physical reality to the positive, and so Reality Construction evolves in multitudinous ways.

Your Personal Reality Field is a result of your Intention, conscious or unconscious, in the creation of Reality Constructs. When you can take <u>conscious</u> responsibility for your creations as a cooperative venture with All That Is, you could say that you are using your Intention in a divine fashion.

To take this further... there is a history on your Earth of the positive use of the human will in tandem with the Divine. As I mentioned in my last book, the great altruistic leaders of your human history knew of a concept we are calling Divine Will. They were experts in the use of Divine Will and took their place alongside of the Divine, acknowledging the collaboration entailed in creating a Personal Reality of worth. In this project, I suggest that you too conceive of your physical incarnation in this timeframe as a cooperative venture with the forces of Nature, the Divine and your Mother Earth.

As a further aid to understanding here in this discussion, and as a way for you to possibly visualize the activity of the Divine Will, I offer the following: consider our theoretical construct of the Subconscious Manifestation Energy Stream, and visualize it as a stream of energy, much as a river is a stream of water. Using this metaphor, can you see, perhaps with your Intuitive Sensing, that just as the elemental energies of your great Earth, "push" water through the soil and dirt and rock until the water makes its way to the other side, further along to its "destination," the human will, Divine Will as we are discussing, as a veritable "force of nature," may push desired thoughts and images per a particular outcome or Reality Construct, across the threshold of potentiality and into the physical? Divine Will is Love guided by your Intention in the moment. It represents the creative energies of All That Is as they are channeled through the consciousness of an inspired human.

Let me remind you that these metaphors are not the ultimate representations of the processes we are describing here, nor will they ever be. They may be seen as bookmarks within my greater theory. They will allow you to continue the study of the new material in a focused way. You may always return to a concept for further meditation, inspiration and study.

The Healing Regimen

The Healing Regimen is a cooperative effort between the practitioner and the Guides in a diagnosis of The Emotional Body. A Blueprint is then made for the creation of a positive reality called Healing. Rituals of Healing are then performed with the application of the various techniques and experiments. The continued application of the Rituals of Healing until The Healing Regimen becomes habitual, creates a positive reality that will sustain itself over time.

Thus, a healing regimen implies regimentation, does it not? Here we are approaching the subject in a very systematic fashion. This is how you get results with these techniques, you see, by creating the Personal Reality Field in purposeful ways. You will not be "sleepwalking" through your life as you may have done in the past. The goal is to achieve conscious awareness in the moment. Then in these moments of awareness, I suggest you enact your Rituals of Healing and purposeful Reality Creation. It is the sequential empowerment of the moments in your existence, that leads in time to the creation of an improved Personal Reality.

This project is really an extended Ritual. If you remember, our definition for Ritual in the context of my new Teaching, is "the consistent requesting of contact and communication with nonphysical beings - Beings of Light." It is all about spirit thought and contact with this stream of communication. Everything in your reality has consciousness and everything may be contacted for communication.

Of course, you may if you wish, continue to heed the communication stream of the ego/intellect, as you have done for perhaps many years in your life. However, if you do, you will in all likelihood merely achieve a recreation of the status quo reality. If you are ill, for example, you may simply recreate a physical body that is ill. I suggest that you do something different here. Experiment with your reality.

The Blueprint

The creation of a structure begins with the drawing-up of a blueprint, illustrating the placement of the materials that will compose the structure. Our Reality Construction of Healing begins with the creation of a Blueprint listing the Techniques, Rituals and Suggestions that we will use to create our Positive Reality. The Blueprint for the Reality Construction of healed bodily states is a "living" document, in that it will change from day to day as you gain information about yourself from your experimentation.

Initially it is necessary to create a potent statement of affirmation that you will build upon to create the Blueprint for The Healing Regimen. The statement should be only a few well-selected words that do indeed epitomize for you the project at hand. It should be a deeply personal and symbolic statement, to the fact that you are identifying as best you can, your current life issue in emotional terms. Again, everything in your created reality is founded in emotion, the emotion of Love. Your health issues are created as you are diverted from Love. With this in mind, you may create your affirmative statement in positive terms, expressing your simple desires with regards to the healing of your body, mind and spirit.

An example may be in order here. Suppose a theoretical subject is experiencing the painful symptoms of a degenerative disease of the musculature of their body. Further, let us say that this subject has experienced a traumatic loss in their recent past. Perhaps a loved-one, such as the father or mother or other family member, has made their Transition in an abrupt manner, through a fast-acting illness that took them within a few weeks, or perhaps through an accident of some sort. Now these traumatic losses are always a surprise to the ego/intellect of those who are left behind. However, as you know, Souls choose the time of departure as well as the circumstances, so the Souls of the departed know that they are merely keeping their appointments in this way.

Yet even though our theoretical subject also knows on a Soul level that their loved-one has simply transferred their energy to the Home Dimension, they are experiencing a Lesson here. The ego/intellect is shocked, outraged, set into a tailspin, so to speak. The grief and other emotions that are triggered by the sudden death serve to take this subject into their Underworld, where they will experience instructional vignettes that illustrate the true nature of the event in a context of the Soul Family. If the subject resists these types of experiences - the perceiving of the true nature of the Soul - symptoms and illness may result. The subject may literally bring to a halt their Soul's progression. This cessation of spiritual growth and fulfillment may result in the outward manifestation of this inner stasis - the atrophy of the musculature of the body.

As you may have noticed, the symptoms and illnesses that humans create within their bodies are often quite literal responses to the perceived traumatic episodes in their lives. But please understand, what one person may perceive as traumatic, another may perceive as business-as-usual. These are deeply personal issues, the creation of imbalances, and should always be addressed as such, taking into account the context of personality, life-style, experiences and all of the other myriad elements that compose the existence of the human.

Now with this in mind, that your health issues are emotionally-based and that some perceived traumatic loss is often involved, using your Inner Senses as you know them, write out a few sentences describing the possible basis for your malady and what it might look like if you were relieved of this malady. Remember, you may always return to this statement to add or subtract material.

For example, if our theoretical subject were to write out a Foundational Statement, it might read as the following:

I sense that I am lost in grief and would like to find my way back to the love and hope I had before the tragedy.

Do you see how this statement frames the Healing Regimen in terms of a journey? Each of you will use your own metaphors and symbols in creating the Foundational Statement. Write it now.

Foundational Statement:

_____

_____

_____

_____

Let us proceed with the Techniques and Rituals that compose The Healing Regimen.

Technique - Consecutive Positive Assessments

The Healing Regimen is a continuous ritual enactment with the elements of our Consecutive Positive Assessments exercise embedded within it. In this exercise you attempt to interpret your moment-to-moment experiences in positive ways. Everything exists within the current moment. Everything that you need to support your Quest for Healing is available to you in your Point of Power, your current Moment Point, right now in this instance. So it is in the moment when you conduct your Rituals of Healing and when you see the results of these Techniques. In the moment is when you get a feel for the creation of successive moments of healing.

With this technique you are attempting to interpret each successive Moment Point as a divine opportunity for positive change. In our book on Soul Evolution we discussed in depth this technique of Consecutive Positive Assessments. Here let me simply state that it is up to you to create this perspective according to what works for you as an individual human, one with particular ways of behaving, one with a certain set of beliefs.

Now briefly, you always have a choice, Dear Reader, regarding what you will experience in the moments of your waking life. You are the creator of your world and the events that occur within your world. So you always have a choice and even a responsibility to make the proper decisions in your moment-to-moment existence to further your life. You must be adequate, in other words, so that you may "live to live another day," in a manner of speaking. Of course, beyond merely living there exists a state of being in which one excels, or develops or grows spiritually, intellectually, and so on. Here in this project, we maintain that to achieve relief from physical illness and the removal of symptoms, one may employ our CPA exercise and "take charge" of the life. By assessing each moment as a joyous and educational experience, the researcher is reprogramming the psyche in a beneficial way. Positive belief change occurs over the long-term application of this technique. Positive realities are created in an intentional way.

Perhaps another example would help. Suppose that our theoretical subject, the human experiencing a disintegration of the musculature of their body, has obtained The Healing Regimen and is trying this Technique. There may be several days of false starts and disruptions of the program. Then one day there is begun a series of moments, perhaps lasting several minutes or even hours, when the subject is truly interpreting their moment-to-moment experiences in positive ways.

In this series of moments, let us say that the subject has perhaps burned the breakfast on the stove. Rather than sink into a depression or scream in anger at the stove, the subject continues to sing a favorite song. In the mental environment of this subject, you might say that the Negative Emotions do not find a place to establish themselves. The singing of the favorite song, perhaps a joyful song, prevents the manipulation of thought energy by the Negative Emotions. The Consecutive Positive Assessments continue even as the song is being sung.

But let us suppose that the subject is then distracted, perhaps by the TV news program as it proclaims the latest tragedy to occur in a far away country. For a moment, the subject may feel a responsibility to the people involved in the tragedy to provide them with a compassionate moment of observation here. Unfortunately, as soon as our subject focuses on the television image, to express their compassion and understanding, the story is ended, and a commercial is run that encourages the viewer to buy products. At this point, the positive mental environment is disrupted. Thoughts relative to things to buy and products of various kinds prevail. The song ceases to be sung.

So the question arises in matters of techniques such as this: "How can I possibly bring conscious awareness to each successive moment in my waking day?" The answer to that, of course, is that it may be difficult to achieve perfection in this assessment exercise. In your physical reality there are numerous diversions, as in our example. There are also natural lapses in consciousness that take you to other dimensions, as we have discussed in our last book. So practically here, I must say, that to the degree that you can accomplish this exercise, you will to that same degree experience positive changes in your Personal Reality Field - you will experience healing within your body, mind and spirit.

Fortunately, simple improvements are what we are marking progress by in this endeavor. You will continuously change course, over the moments of your existence, making your simple improvements, until gradually you are experiencing the voyage as a positive habit of thought, feeling and manifestation.

Technique - Distracting the Ego/Intellect

Your ego/intellect is an expert in the creation of status quo realities. It always begins its work on awakening after your sleeping times, whenever that might be. As you open your eyes, there is a tendency for the ego/intellect to take charge IMMEDIATELY. It is your job to remember that your regimen will begin or continue at that particular time, and circumvent the strategies of the ego/intellect to control your Reality Creation agendas.

You do this by distracting the ego/intellect. This is a divine distraction. You divert your attention from the mundane to the Divine. This is simply a personal reminder from your Soul Self that you are supported on a wave of ecstasy just below the surface of consciousness. We have described this feeling state in our last two books. You are supported; you are endorsed; you are Loved. You do not need to recreate the status quo reality of suffering, illness and other negative states. You may also use your Energy Personality and other Guides *(See the experiment at the end of this chapter. mf)* to help remind you of your Sacred Quest in these moments.

However, if you are like most people, your ego/intellect will not enjoy these attempts to divert the manifestation energies toward the Divine. The ego/intellect may flood your consciousness with Negative Emotions, traumatic memories, reminders of financial peril etc. You may experience a sudden fear that you are taking these explorations too far, perhaps wandering into "the danger zone." Religious conditioning may serve to bring doubt to mind. You may feel that perhaps you should go to church soon or speak to a priest. Of course you may do these things. You have free will. But might I suggest that you are now acting as your own intermediary? You are bridging the physical and subtle realms with your awareness. Just as the magician, the shaman, the witch does, you are acting as your own intermediary between the physical and the Divine.

My advice to you, when you are experiencing these responses from the ego/intellect, is to intervene with your Intention, and possibly with the assistance of your Guides, and divert your attention back to the Divine. It is really just a matter of choice in the moment. You are choosing from the perspective of the Soul Self, a path of improved Reality Creation.

Technique - Suspending Disbelief

Another technique the researcher may use is the suspension of disbelief. This is the divine perspective that is necessary for you to CONTINUE to create moments of healing within your Personal Reality Field. When you first meet with success at creating a cessation of symptoms, for example, through your Healing Talk or other strategies, your rational mind will surely be amazed. If you are at that moment perceiving through the ego/intellect, you may "not believe your eyes," and ascribe the transformation to something other than your Divine Will. This may serve to short circuit the healing process. Doubt is interjected into the mix and so faith or courage becomes compromised. Rather I suggest that at the moment of cessation of symptoms, be joyous and amazed, knowing that you have succeeded in that moment with co-creating your reality with All That Is toward the healing of your body. There is a sense of humility you can muster here, and yet still marvel at your powers of manifestation. It is a balance you may achieve between humility and charisma, between supreme confidence and wishful thinking.

Dear Reader, you are already expert at the suspension of disbelief. When you enjoy a book or a movie or other dramatic presentation, you are immersing yourself in the media and you are letting go of the skeptical aspect of your personality for the time being. As you create the story in your imagination that is suggested by the words in the book or the scenes in the movie or on the stage, you are submitting your inner self to the influences of the story. This you have done countless times, no doubt, when you were a child listening to fairy tales, for example. As well, you are continuing this tradition as an adult when you experience stories of any type. So this use of the imagination is a very natural one for you. It is the basis for all of your creative endeavors as human beings, including the very basic practice of Reality Creation.

Rituals of Healing

As do all of our exercises and experiments in this new material, The Healing Regimen begins with the Ritual of Sanctuary *(See Book Two. mf)*. This act of protection and Sanctuary I suggest you perform in the morning as you rise for the day and at regular intervals throughout your waking day.

In the beginning I would also suggest that you use your Intention and perseverance to cut your affiliations - your metaphysical, psychic connections - to any Gestalts of Consciousness that feed to you negative information, such as symptom-creation strategies, dire predictions, negative prognosis information etc. The "voices" of these Energy Forms are the energetic supports onto which you fasten the body of your created reality. So it is very important for you, on your Healing Quest, to heed the voices of ONLY those Energy Bodies that may assist you in bringing balance to your physical, mental and spiritual being. These benign and beneficial energies are easy to recognize. As you attempt to find these "voices," you may notice that your emotional state is transformed as you "tune-in" to the Loving energies.

The Metaphorical Tools

It is within your power as co-creator with All That Is to use your Divine Will to create more appropriate realities for yourself. You may do this with the Metaphorical Tools of various types. In our book on Soul Evolution we described one such tool: the Radio Dial Metaphor. Let us again describe the activity of this magical dial. This is simply a visualized dial, possibly modeled on a dial you have seen on one of your radios or other electronic devices. By turning the physical radio dial, different radio frequencies are accessed and different radio stations are contacted. By turning the visualized dial on our visualized radio, the researcher "tunes-in" to the Energy Bodies that compose nonphysical reality.

This is a Metaphorical Tool used in a Ritual way. Time after time, as these connections and communications with Beings of Light are established, it becomes a habitual act. I might add, that it also becomes easier to make these connections, the more you use your Metaphorical Tools.

With the dial, for example, you may discover your Guides, learn their names, and consult with other Gestalts of Consciousness that may assist you. Through the use of this tool, using your Inner Senses in an Intentional way, you may safely observe and study the disease-producing Idea Constructs. With the Metaphorical Tools you create a "protective barrier" between your consciousness and the Idea Constructs that support the malady.

Of course you may use any Metaphorical Tools that you have already established for your use in your past experiments. Or you may develop your own set of tools to assist you in your project. So that you might create an Inner Screen, for example, onto which you may project various images or scenes for study. You may create for your use a transportation device of your choosing, one that may take you to various locations in the past, present and future and in both the physical and nonphysical worlds. It is up to you to use your imagination to create tools that can serve your particular needs. Now let us begin the experimentation that will furnish you with data to create the Blueprint for The Healing Regimen.

Experiment - Calling In Your Guides
Hypothesis: the nonphysical beings may assist you in the healing regimen.

As a nonphysical being in service to mankind at this time, I offer my help to you in your Quest for Healing and Balance. As well, you may have already contacted your Guides, such as the Energy Personality and others to assist you. If you have yet to create these relationships, I suggest that you continue with The Healing Regimen "as if" you were in contact and communication with your Guides. Let me elaborate for just a moment...

Part One
Perform your Ritual of Sanctuary
Consider your powerful imagination. Now the imagination is the great creative force in your system that assists you in your creation of Reality Constructs. The emotional energy that "fuels" this Reality Construction, as I have stated, is based in Love, a very potent emotion. Now here in this instance, in your protected state of Sanctuary that you are experiencing, can you imagine with your great creative intelligence, a relationship with what you might call a Spirit Guide? Can you sense the powerful current of Love and compassion that supports and sustains this relationship? Stay with this for

a few moments. Images may come to mind for you, suggesting characters from your childhood, possibly representing "imaginary playmates." Loving characters from your mythologies may appear in the mind's eye. I suggest you go with the flow here, knowing that there is Loving Intent, and envision your Guide into being. Ask for the name of the Guide and it will come to you. The name may have a nonsensical quality to it or it may be rather mundane. Accept the name if you intuitively feel it is right. This is a preliminary exercise here. You are not seeking perfection, simply progress in this endeavor. Whatever comes to you in so far as name and appearance and emotional content is quite sufficient. Honor this process and accept what you are creating with All That Is in this moment.

This is simply a way for you to conduct the necessary behaviors and Idea Constructs into reality formations in the Third Dimension. You usually do not value something as real, unless you see a beginning, middle and end to it in your Physical Reality. This is why your Guides, even though they are seeking your contact, do not suddenly appear to you "out of the blue." Your Guides do not wish to scare you, in other words. This is the beginning of the manifestation of your Guides into your Personal Reality Field, and in a sense, you will "believe them into existence."

Findings - Take a few moments to document your experiences in contacting your guides.

Part Two

The second part of this experiment deals with the calling in of your various Guides and Helpers, for those of you who have already established these relationships.

Perform your Ritual of Sanctuary

You are in your state of Sanctuary. From this perspective it may be easy for you to envision your Guides as they appear on your mental screen perhaps, and what skills each may employ in assisting you in The Healing Regimen. Your Energy Personality, for example, may be asked to assist you in remembering that you are embarked upon a path of positive moment-to-moment assessments of your experiences. You might ask, that, should you lapse into the robotic trance or negative ruminations common to many of you in your system, you would be reminded, possibly by some specific sensory cue from your Energy Personality, to awaken and proceed with the Rituals of Healing. You may have specific Helpers that you rely upon in matters of healing and balance. I suggest you call them in to assist you in the day-to-day program of positive assessment and Reality Creation. The Guides may provide you with the ongoing Loving emotional energy required to sustain The Healing Regimen. In essence, here you are attempting to create a divine state of consciousness long term. You are asking for the assistance of your divine Guides, and as they help you through each successive moment in The Healing Regimen, you will feel the beneficial energies and effects upon your physical body.

Findings - As the project moves forward, document your experiences in accessing and utilizing your Guides.

Experiment - Reading The Emotional Body
Hypothesis: the emotional body displays the causes and cures of all maladies.

Now let us attempt to "read" The Emotional Body. You will be attempting to assess, with your Auric Vision, the energy signatures of the various imbalances and cures inherent in the Auric Display.

Perform Your Ritual of Sanctuary

First, please attempt to embody a deep state of relaxation. You may accomplish this by focusing on your breathing for just a few moments. You may also stretch your body in your particular fashion that leads to relaxation and a focus on the inner world. Use whatever methods you have perfected in your experimentation.

Now what we are attempting here, as in all experimental research in this new Teaching of mine, is nothing less than the entering into the Trance State, as you call it. This state of consciousness is simply the mental environment of your Soul Self. Here you bridge the inner to the outer worlds with your awareness. You fine-tune the perceptive tools - your Inner Senses - with your Intention to achieve the precise focus of awareness that YOU require to accomplish your goals.

The perceived representation of The Emotional Body may encompass the majority of the physical body, but is centered, as I said, within the heart region. The "reading" of The Emotional Body has a visual component, yet it may also be a felt sensation, as in a sense of tingling or other energy signatures within your own body. You may also experience it as a "heard" vibrational message in the manner of a song. These sensings may come to you as images and full visions, possibly composed of persons or animals in various roles, acting out various scenes for your education and enjoyment. The dramatizations may be sensed on the inward eye, though the eyes may indeed be open. The visionary state permits these contradictions - feeling the pulse of visualized scenes or hearing the songs of manifested illnesses and their sources.

The Auric Vision is the Inner Sense representation to your mental awareness of the health issue in its totality. This potent Idea Construct or Gestalt of Consciousness exists as a holographic reference that contains everything you as the Healer require to diagnose and bring balance to your own body or the body of your subject. Each of you will sense and interpret this information in your individual ways.

This Auric Vision may come to you quite quickly, just as you enter your state of awareness, or it may take several minutes for you to focus on your Inner Senses and achieve a diagnosis and perceive possible cures. You may need to "sleep on it" and receive the bulk of the information in the dream state, for assessment, diagnosis and curative measures to be achieved on awakening. These are matters of individual preferences with regards to the healing process. Do what serves best your needs or the needs of your subject.

Some techniques that may be useful:

Use your hands to fan around the body, "feeling" for any anomalies of energy vibration. You may do this literally, with your physical hands and make passes around your own body or the body of your subject, or you may do this in the visualized form, using your imagination.

Project your consciousness into your body or the body of your subject, to search from within it as a miniature explorer.

Listen to the narrative of the subject and derive from these words, the messages from the Energy Bodies that will serve to direct you to the cause of the difficulties. This narrative may serve to bring to your mind a visual or other sensory dramatization that holds the diagnosis information in symbolic or literal form.

When you are working on your own healing, simply attempt to tune-in to your inner ruminations. These messages are the supports of the Gestalts of Consciousness we are calling disease process. Now also within this inner dialogue are messages from Beings of Light. These suggestions may have come from your future probable existences *(see experiment at end of this chapter. mf)* or from other Guides who are attempting to assist you in your Healing Journey. Simply put, here in this experiment you are tuning-in the healing states and tuning-out the Gestalts of Consciousness that support the disease.

Now illness is a Lesson that your Soul Self has "arranged" for you to experience in physical form, yet it is possible to heal yourself if you can learn the Lesson in other ways. For example: suppose on reading your Light Body you discover that the "reason" for your diabetes, is an imbalance in The Emotional Body. You are having difficulty accepting and processing "the sweetness that life has to offer." This manifests as physical illness in a very literal way. You may heal yourself by learning how to accept and transmit the sweetness of life. You needn't suffer unto death from the illness. So it is essential that the underlying "cause" of the malady be addressed or the difficulty may come back in another form, as in a physical, mental or spiritual malady of some sort. These are matters of belief revision. This subject will be explored next.

Findings - Document your Findings from this ongoing experiment.

Experiment - Belief Revision
Hypothesis: beliefs that support disease may adapt to support healing.

Every thought you entertain within your mental sphere seeks to create itself within the physical or other dimensions, according to the templates of your beliefs about what is possible. Your thoughts of creating a healed physical body, therefore, create your potentially healed body within Dimensional-Realms that exist in probability, just as your thoughts of disease and symptoms create your malady. As you continue to focus in your Ritual fashion upon the creation of healing and balance, you continually "feed" these pre-manifestation templates with "energy" in the form of Consciousness Units. This ongoing energetic support serves to move the potential reality from the probable Dimensional-Realms into the physical Third Dimension. As you witness your co-creation of healing, your beliefs will adapt to these astounding new perceptions. The probability of healing becomes possible and finally inevitable. Your beliefs may change from skeptical to ardently supportive in this process.

Knowing this, what do you suppose the healer "sees" when they first look upon the healing or balancing that is taking place within their own system? Now this can be rather tricky to describe and to comprehend. In this case, the healer would INTEND to observe a healing transformation within the biological system. As you know, all of physical reality is a product of consciousness. In the case of the healing of the body, mind or spirit it is precisely the same. Here, your attitude is very important. Your conscious Intent is the most important element in this proceeding. So that when you observe your emerging reality, let us say upon first awakening from sleep, your conscious Intent is that you are very naturally and easily co-creating your emerging reality according to the Blueprint of healing you have decided upon in this project. *(See Blueprint section pge. 138. mf)*

As you master the co-creation of your Personal Reality Field, and you bring conscious awareness to the task at hand, the essentially magical act of healing becomes internalized. Beyond a particular point, you need not even think about it, for it has become automatic. Your beliefs will adapt and you will become more certain of your skills in the creation of the healing moment. You are redrawing your Blueprint for health, here. You are redefining the templates of creation by making the creation of the healing moment habitual.

Now... identify and list beliefs you feel may be contributing to the creation and perpetuation of the malady. This material may take the form of a narrative or simply a list of short declarative statements.

129

When you feel you have something to work with in this experiment, consider the divine opposites of these statements or a positive counter to the narrative. Write them down next to each other.

Perform your Ritual of Sanctuary

You are in your protected state. Using your Inner Senses, relax with your written material and occasionally read out loud or to yourself the statements and their divine counterparts. Here your intent may be in support emotionally of the positive statements and nonsupport emotionally of the malady-producing statements of beliefs. So you are making a declaration here that you are changing your beliefs. You are withdrawing the emotional energy, the emotional charge, from the one, and you are empowering with your emotional energy the other - the health-creating and sustaining statements or beliefs. The positive suggestions of healthful support will become internalized allowing you to release the malady-creating beliefs. As this occurs you may find that your symptoms change to reflect the changing beliefs.

Disease and symptoms serve very specific purposes, you see. They are the direct reflection of interior processes. They are the physical expression of nonphysical concepts and images.

Findings - Note your beliefs and their adaptations over time.

Experiment - Healing Talk
Hypothesis: positive suggestions help to create positive realities.

My friend Mark here has recently explored the work of a premier hypnotist living in your timeframe. This fellow truly explores the magical component of Healing Talk, as we are calling it. He has discovered that the suggestions you give yourself continuously, your "inner dialogue," or whatever you wish to call this conversation, are indeed very influential in your co-creation of the Personal Reality Field. Everything is suggestion, you see. All is the work of Gestalts of Consciousness.

Let me digress... we have spoken at length in this manuscript on the great value in "listening" to the suggestions of your Loving Guides. These suggestions often take the form of positive thoughts, feelings and images sensed within your mental environment. It feels, at these times of contact, that you may be experiencing a divine intervention of sorts, for the experiences of the preceding moments may have been anything other than positive and Loving. Your preceding experiences may have been very negative and challenging. Perhaps what you have done then is you have put out a call to your Guides to assist you in your Reality Creation, and they have done so. In this way, you have asked for assistance from your Guides and they have responded "right when you needed it most."

Another way to experience this state of contact with the Divine in an ongoing manner, is to "plant" the positive suggestions within your consciousness purposely, so that over time you are training yourself to experience your world in a positive way, with continuous contact with the Divine. You then recreate your reality in a positive fashion. The creation of positive realities becomes habitual, replacing the habitual creation of negative or mundane realities. This purposeful guiding of the human mentality through speech is the basis of all your healing systems on your Earth. From the aboriginal shaman to your modern medicine practitioner, all have used Healing Talk for support in the healing process.

Perform your Ritual of Sanctuary

This experiment is similar to the preceding one, with a subtle difference. Now relax your body using your preferred techniques. The products of your Belief Revisioning are the affirmative statements you may use to counter the negative ruminations that support the creation of your mundane existence. Ideally you would have committed the affirmative statements or suggestions to memory. If not, have your suggestions written out on a piece of paper to read when you are at your preferred state of relaxation. The next step is to read your affirmative statements to yourself while you are in Trance, or perhaps record the statements for playback while you are in your relaxed state. Over time, if you are diligent, the positive healing statements will supplant the negative ruminations that support the malady.

Findings - Document your Findings rigorously in creating Healing Talk that counters your negative ruminations.

Experiment - Consulting Your Future Healed Self
Hypothesis: you can receive advice from your future healed self.

Perform your Ritual of Sanctuary

This experiment would be a form of "back engineering," as Mark has described it to me. For example: as you visit this future healed self, using your visualized transport, you might ask yourself, "What am I doing differently now that has perhaps helped me achieve this healed state?" Make a list of what comes to mind. You are indeed in that moment of contact, receiving information from a probable future self that is experiencing a healed state. This information gathering may take the form of an informal interview. Have a list of questions prepared prior to the experiment. If you are sufficiently comfortable in Trance that you will not be distracted by reading your questions, have the questions available to refer to during the interview.

Now... this is your most effective advisor, your future healed self. This information from your future self may take the form of nonsense. You may, for example, be advised to perform an absurd gesture, motion or such thing. This does not make sense to your Third-Dimensional ego, for it may seem embarrassing, silly etc. If you feel that you are in contact with your Guides, that you are guided by them and you are in contact with your future healed self, my advice is to take the advice of this Energy Body. Perform the silly gesture. Do the embarrassing behavior. Obviously, we would not wish to harm anyone, including the practitioner, in taking this advice.

You may, using your Inner Senses, perceive this future healed self and you might ask questions of this self and receive the telepathic responses that you may integrate into your Healing Regimen. These responses may come in symbolic form. Again, using your intuitive faculties, interpret these messages and act on them or not. Of course you have free will here, as do you in all facets of your existence, and you may act accordingly.

Findings - Write down the answers you are receiving or in another way document this information from your future self.

Experiment - Creating the Panacea
Hypothesis: you may empower anything with healing attributes.

You know that, beyond growing a new limb, there is nothing in your Personal Reality Field that cannot be changed provided you create the "conditions" for change that are required. Period. These conditions or requirements for manifestation are two fold: First - you require an intensity of desire and emotion that supersedes the level of emotion that creates and sustains the current reality. Second - your personal beliefs must expand to include the POSSIBILITY for the creation of the changes you wish to experience. The level of emotion that sustains or maintains your manifested reality within your Personal Reality Field may be thought of, for purposes of this explanation, as nominal or "just enough" to sustain your reality as you know it. This nominal output of emotional manifestation energy is an ongoing product of what you would term your "unconscious" or "subconscious." You are not aware of it, in other words, as this creative energy stream does its work just beyond your field of awareness.

Now let us apply this theoretical concept to healing. As you know, Natural Healing is our term for the use of natural products - oils, waters, empowered objects of various types - in the healing and balancing of the human body. We have suggested to readers also in our last book, that the application of these treatments to the various illnesses of the human body, need not be in a one-to-one correspondence. In other words, it is not necessary to use a specific oil or water to assist in the healing of a specific malady. You need not seek out the specific curative. We have suggested that you have the power, within your creative consciousness, to imbue anything with the curative energy for the healing and balancing of the body. With this in mind, let us create an experiment in exploring the effects of the panacea.

Now a panacea is literally a cure-all. In your time it is often referred to in mythological terms, for your medical model cannot hold the concept of a cure-all within it.

Perform your Ritual of Sanctuary

Relax your body. Now the cure-all may be a physical product of some sort, as in an oil, water or perhaps a physical object such as a stone or artifact. It may also be visualized. As you enter your relaxed state of Trance, perhaps holding the panacea substance or object in your hand, your goal is to use your Intention to energize the panacea with curative powers. This panacea will be empowered with all of the healing energies resident within the Gestalt of Consciousness we are calling Spontaneous Healing. You are simply accepting the transmission of the energy flow from this Energy Body into your physical body. You will then, using your Intention again, direct the healing energy into the panacea for storage. This healing energy will not lose its potency while in the panacea. You may use your panacea in ways you see fit, to treat the malady.

You may sense this data bank of healing influences called Spontaneous Healing in any way you wish. Perhaps you will tune-in with your Metaphorical Tools, guided by the Loving energies emitted by this Energy Body. Perhaps you will "travel" to this Gestalt of Consciousness in a metaphorical vehicle of some sort, or simply within the Astral Form, as you call it. The nonphysical body is always available for conveying your consciousness to any location in nonphysical and physical reality. Simply imagine it to be and it will be so.

Findings - Document your successes and challenges in creating and using the panacea.

The Regimen Continues

You are required to learn your own Lessons in physical reality. The nonphysical beings are not permitted to interfere. Now this is why I must be rather vague in my presentation to you of these Rituals and Techniques. You are to work out the particulars on your own, and by so doing, gain the expertise and Value Fulfillment entailed in this project. Some of you will be satisfied to obtain modest results in this endeavor, while others will accept nothing less than "perfection." These are your beliefs that determine "success" in this or any of our other projects. It is all a matter of your free will choice.

The Blueprint

consists of the studious application of the Rituals of Healing, the Techniques and your personal Findings to the issue at hand.

CPA	Consecutive Positive Assessments
DTEI	Distracting the Ego/Intellect
SD	Suspending Disbelief
MT	Metaphorical Tools
CIYG	Calling in Your Guides
RTEB	Reading The Emotional Body
BR	Belief Revision
HT	Healing Talk
CYFHS	Consulting Your Future Healed Self
CTP	Creating the Panacea

7 DAY CALENDAR

At the end of the day, assess on a scale of 1 to 7 your use of the Rituals and Techniques suggested in The Healing Regimen.

1 - Very little Use   2 - Some Use   3 - Moderate Use   4 - Regular Use

5 - Consistent Use   6 - Concerted Use   7 - Very focussed Use

	M	T	W	T	F	S	S
CPA							
DTEI							
SD							
MT							
CIYG							
RTEB							
BR							
HT							
CYFHS							
CTP							

CHAPTER SEVEN

Spiritual Prosperity

Dialogue - Faith
6/15/05 5:20 PM

Mark: I have 10 minutes on a topic of your choice.
Seth: Mark, the topic for this brief session is faith. Faith is the great power behind the manifestation process. Faith implies positive, shall we say, "divine" motivations. Can you Mark, relax your vigilant observations of your self-created reality? Go with the flow. Look behind the scenes of your life drama and see what is really on your mind. See what you are really creating with your positive thoughts.

Dialogue - Prosperity Issues
6/24/06 8:26 PM

Seth: Do you see that I am directing this at you, my friend?
Mark: Yes Seth. I'm beginning to get the picture.

Spiritual Prosperity

We have titled this chapter Spiritual Prosperity to again challenge your beliefs about what is and is not spiritual. Everything is literally made of spirit. Everything in your world is spiritual, therefore. Spirit is Light. Spirit is energy. You are on the Earth currently to learn how to use energy to create your world in an improved fashion. From this premise we shall move forward.

Our Spiritual Prosperity Program will allow you to transform your beliefs and ideas about abundance. If you are experiencing a lack of necessities, you will be empowered to alter your perspective in a necessary fashion to reveal The Abundant Universe. Now this Abundant Universe is always there for you to experience. It is a probable manifestation from the field of limitless probabilities before you. Your focus upon the positive elements within your field of perception is the path to creating and experiencing The Abundant Universe. You may remember this as the Consecutive Positive Assessments technique from the last chapter. In the Spiritual Prosperity Program we shall avail ourselves of the techniques and experiments used in The Healing Regimen.

Gestalts of Consciousness and Prosperity

Prosperity, The Abundant Universe, havingness are all simply "states of mind." They are also Gestalts of Consciousness as we have defined the term in this manuscript. As Consciousness Units are manipulated by consciousness over the millennia in the creation of realities, templates of creation are "agreed upon" to serve as the blueprints for the creation of Reality Constructs of all types. Those states of consciousness that you may call "poverty" and "just getting by," serve as the blueprints for self - the Soul Self - to create an ongoing less-than-prosperous life.

This may appear to you as overly simplified. Dear Reader, it truly is quite simple. This is the basic dynamic of Reality Creation in the Third Dimension. I have also referred to this act of creation as a matter of "alliance" with Entities of various kinds. It is all the same here. Reality Creation occurs at the point where your Intention, your focus, your consciousness, your spirit meets the Third Dimension. Period.

Do you notice how matters of worthiness and guilt do NOT enter into this discussion of the basics of manifestation? The human being in the throes of feeling unworthy, of feeling guilty, of feeling cursed interjects these Negative Emotions into the blueprints of the Reality Creation project. This could be your current existence, for example. As the human degrades, in a sense, this basic template of creation, the GOC we are calling The Abundant Universe is transformed over time into one that creates a life of "just getting by" or even one of "abject poverty."

The Abundant Universe is your baseline reality. You are born within The Abundant Universe. Over time you have a tendency to make this GOC "your own" by personalizing it with your Negative Emotions. You do this for purposes of dramatizing your Lessons in physical reality. You are aided by members of your Soul Family in this endeavor. Your main task in creating Spiritual Prosperity is to work with your Soul Family to perceive and create The Abundant Universe.

The Abundant Universe

The Abundant Universe exists, as does any other potent GOC, as a holographic entity within your collective consciousness. Both past and future memories of this state are released in ecstatic dreaming. Your myths of paradise and your stories of the Garden of Eden and other highly idealized Utopian constructs, are fragments of this GOC that serve to remind you of how pleasant physical reality can be. You feel a great sense of longing when engaged in these visionary activities, as though a priceless element of existence has been lost forever. This, however, is OVER-dramatizing the issue. (humorously) The Abundant Universe is there before you, where it always is, where it has always been, in your terms. The perceptual blinders we are calling the Negative Emotions serve to block your view of this paradise.

We have used terms such as calcification, hardening of the vision, etc. to explain the process of the human creating the self-imposed "blindness" within the personal consciousness. Knowing this, I am certain that you may grasp the simplicity of succeeding in this enterprise Spiritual Prosperity. It is a matter of waking-up to your true reality. It is a matter of facing your Lessons with Courage and Loving Understanding. It is a matter of remembering paradise and then recreating it in the moment.

Money Value Spirit

What is money in your system? Let us attempt a general definition for our program. Money is the currency that you trade for the material needs of living. For the most part, you must earn the money in some way, through employment in an occupation, for example. Naturally I am aware that some of my readers have inherited wealth, or are in some way benefited by the work or efforts of others, without the need for employment themselves. There are myriad possibilities here. Money is obtained through countless means. Money acts as a medium of exchange, as you say.

Example of Value Fulfillment

Now my concept of Value Fulfillment enters here, as you might well expect. Money has value, I am sure you will agree. Yet please allow me to describe for you the "spiritual" basis of this value. An example for illustration: my associate Mark receives a check from one of our readers in exchange for a book or some other item. When Mark takes the check in his hands from the envelope, he experiences an emotional response. These emotions may run the gamut from positive to negative depending on the context, the conditions of existence, you see. Remember, it is a process of creating realities from emotional states of consciousness, this Third-Dimensional existence. The emotions of Mark, and indeed of all of you, vary in type and degree throughout your waking hours. This is quite obvious to you I am sure.

Now let us say that our subject here, as he opens the envelope and examines the check, is prepared for a pleasant experience. He has received checks from readers before. It is an emotional pleasure to receive these checks. As he examines this check, he is viewing his reality through the perspective of The Abundant Universe. He is appreciating the "magical" appearance of money in his mailbox. There is a history here, in other words, that he remembers, and in the moment he is grateful, appreciative, quite pleased.

Please observe that while our subject is perceiving through the perspective of The Abundant Universe, he is also strengthening this perspective through his appreciation and gratitude in the moment. Remember that in the Moment Point you are "priming the pump" with positive images and ideas that will set the stage for further demonstrations of The Abundant Universe in your perceived future. The creation of this positive reality of The Abundant Universe is becoming habitual.

On the other hand, just for the sake of argument (humorously), suppose for a moment that our subject is not necessarily perceiving from a grateful, magical, abundant perspective. Suppose that, moments before opening the envelope containing the check, he had an encounter with someone that "caused" him to become anxious, fearful, angry. These Negative Emotions, further let us say, combine within his psyche to create a potent quite toxic brew of ingratitude and disdain that will color his Reality Creation efforts, at least for the short term - for the next few minutes or hours. You may possibly guess what might be the result of our subject's opening the envelope containing the check. Certainly we might not expect gratitude or an appreciation of the magical nature of the Universe. Most probably we may expect a less than healthy response from him, for he has set himself up to create negative realities by succumbing to the energies of negativity.

Thirdly, may we take it for granted that our subject IS learning Lessons of gratitude, acceptance and the other virtues of humankind? If we may, let us also assume that he is actively involved in learning these Lessons consciously and has identified the negative GOC resident in his psyche, one we might call Ingratitude. Knowing that he has the power to "change his mind" with his Intent, he uses his Divine Will to create Loving Understanding and Courage out of anxiety, fearfulness and anger. Thus, upon opening the envelope and observing the check, he is well-prepared to experience gratitude, perceive The Abundant Universe and perhaps marvel at the magical nature of Reality Creation.

In the first case, our subject is appreciating the value of the magical aspect of money creation. In the second case, he is concerned with experiencing the value of Negative Emotions and those realities created through these emotions. In the third case he is experiencing the value of empowerment that comes with awakening in the moment to his Reality

Creation agenda, and then using his powers of creation to change that agenda. In all cases, he is learning SPIRITUAL Lessons that will add to the experiencing of his Entity and All That Is.

Prosperity and Simultaneous Lives

Now all of you are on Earth to learn a literal <u>lifetime</u> of Lessons. The Lessons of value, abundance, money are often related to matters of authority, SELF-worth and personal power. You might say that the person experiencing a lifetime of lack has most probably experienced emotional injuries in these domains, certainly in the current existence, and also in other Simultaneous Lives. In this way, all perceived negative conditions are truly systemic, representing a focus by the Soul Self on the injurious Gestalts of Consciousness lending their creative energy and direction to the creation of the negative conditions in all of the participating Reincarnational Existences. It is indeed a group effort here, as it is in all matters of the individual human experiencing their Lessons - positive or negative - in any particular lifetime.

An example of this multidimensional group effort is in order. Imagine a Soul Self, an Entity composed of, shall we say, several thousand Simultaneous Lives, as well as innumerable probable existences. Each of these Selves, additionally, is unaware of the others. They are each individually living their lives in different eras, in different circumstances. Let us suppose that of these many lives, a small percentage is experiencing what you might call "wealth" or a perception of The Abundant Universe. To simplify, let us say that the remaining lives are experiencing less than favorable conditions. Now the lives experiencing lack "support" one another on the subtle levels via the Telepathic Network. Through impulses received telepathically from their fellow impoverished selves, the poor ones are given instruction and advice, in a sense, on how to create an impoverished existence. Now this is how it works under all circumstances for you in your world. As I said, you and all of your lives are learning Lessons. You support one another in learning your Lessons via these impulses sent and received on the subtle levels.

In these matters of the Soul Self and the learning of Lessons there is no judgment. There is no experiencing of the emotional complex of guilt on these levels of interaction. The Soul Self has a mandate, you might say, that is emotion-free, to assist in the creation of the reincarnational dramas and comedies for the Simultaneous Lives. It is the individual lives themselves that bring the emotional element into the mix for learning purposes.

Religious Conditioning and Faith

Dear Reader, I believe that a spiritual practice of prosperity is necessary to assist those in need of reconciling their religious or spiritual beliefs with their desires for material wealth. Within this spiritual practice of abundance it is perfectly "OK" to entertain thoughts of acquiring material possessions, engaging in desired behaviors with other humans, and so on. However, these thoughts or visualizations will be created within a different mental environment than you may be used to. For is it not true that there may be a lingering element of suspicion within your consciousness when you are "hoping" for your financial affairs to improve, that it most probably will not turn out the way you would like? The lingering doubt that you may be engaging in desperation and foolishness, or worse yet, "the work of the devil" - the sin of avarice - may have held you back in your efforts at manifesting abundance. It is true, that in matters of conscious co-creation, the focus must be steady and unswerving with an element of hopeful expectation powering the exercise.

So faith enters the discussion. Here I would ask you to drop any negative connotations that you may have attached to the word faith. When we suggest you embody the state of faith, we would hope (humorously) that no symbols or emotions will be recalled that will keep you away from what you are attempting to create. Some examples of these counterproductive ideas are: fear of punishment by religious figures, thoughts that faith is a religious concept that will not work for you etc. We are redefining the concept of empowered spirituality here. As in other experiments and exercises in this new material, we are asking you to change your beliefs and ideas about what is possible. In this case, the object is to empower the word faith with an energy of creation that is Loving, accepting, Courageous.

Perhaps a short example may help you. Consider the bird, the rock, the tree, the mountain. Do they worry what the future will bring? I suggest they do not. All of these quite conscious elements LIVE within the moment, experiencing the existence as providing all that is required. The human, on the other hand, complicates matters in the matter of existence and brings fear, worry and doubt into the equation.

Let us say then that our faith, our trust, our hope in this theory of Reality Creation, is in essence the simple Loving expectation, in the moment, of consciousness. We may even go so far as to say that the human embodying this faith we are describing, is utilizing within the moment, the creative potencies of All That Is. Now the human would do well to emulate the bird, the rock, the tree in this embodying of faith. Look around you and see how the various living and "inert" compositions are sustained within the moment. The future and the past do not exist. There is only the current moment of existence for consciousness.

Perception of Lack

The key emotional support that the human brings to prevent the clear perception of The Abundant Universe is LACK. The perception of lack, emotionally experienced over time, creates and sustains the state of consciousness called poverty. In those who create lives of "just getting by," this emotional tone is somewhat pronounced. In those who create lives of abject poverty, it is pervasive. The emotional Idea Construct of lack is the electromagnetic core to which the varying Reality Constructs that compose the Personal Reality of the human experiencing poverty are attracted. Briefly, if you see lack wherever you look, you are conceiving and perpetuating lack wherever you go.

Now before we continue with this explanation, please allow me to explain again the process of the Soul Self as it creates a life of Lessons. Thus far, my description of the self-created reality of poverty may seem to be quite heartless, a matter of "blaming the victim." After all, how does one explain the many innocent children living in famine-afflicted countries? How can I possibly suggest that these children CHOSE their current existences? Dear Reader, remember that the Soul Self sends a fragment of itself into the body of the baby and then creates Lessons without guilt or other Negative Emotions. Also, on deep levels of understanding, the baby also knows and accepts the conditions of the coming life. Yes, it is dramatic, the hundreds of thousands of humans who die under these miserable conditions. Yet that is the point here. The Soul is dramatizing for the Entity and All That Is, as well as the subject, these difficult Lessons.

Again, without generalizing too much here, I can tell you that many of these short lives are experienced by Souls who have reached the end of their incarnations on Earth. They are ready for the peaceful and Loving realities of other systems. They are quite enthused about "going out of the loop," in a sense, with a great flourish - the short, dramatic existence of a child in a poor country, let us say, who seems to be truly a victim. In the greater perspective of the Soul Self, it is just the opposite. These children are creating their lives through great bravery and Loving acceptance. They are not victims.

Lack Continued

I have just suggested that the human experiencing an absence of havingness has quite probably experienced emotional distress within the domains of personal power and authority. These injuries occur within the Simultaneous Lives and are re-experienced by the human via impulses sent to them from these lives. The human that acts upon these suggestions will create more unfortunate experiences in their ongoing life. Over time, the state of consciousness we are referring to as lack "solidifies" as the recreation of states of lack becomes habitual. It seems there is no hope here. The subject may feel they were born to be poor, to be without. Like depression, the entire field of the Personal Reality is colored by these negative conditions. And in a reciprocal fashion, the outer environment reflects the inner state of emotional injury. You create your own reality, you see. You have effectively created a belief in the inevitability of poverty. You have created poverty through the template of this belief. Because the emotional tone of lack is pervasive in the Personal Reality Field, you habitually will choose only those thoughts, images, behaviors that will recreate the status quo. Thus lack endures.

I have painted a bleak picture for you, Dear Reader. (humorously) Now I shall present some Techniques and Experiments that will assist you in your Spiritual Prosperity Program, at whatever level of lack you find yourself.

Definition of Spiritual Prosperity

The Spiritual Prosperity Program is a cooperative effort between the practitioner and the Guides in a diagnosis of The Emotional Body. A Blueprint is then made for the creation of a positive reality called Prosperity. Rituals of Prosperity are then performed with the application of the various techniques and experiments. The continued application of the Rituals of Prosperity until the manifestation becomes habitual, creates a positive reality that will sustain itself over time.

The Blueprint

You are preparing to create a positive reality of abundance. It would be a good idea to create a personalized program for the attainment of this goal. As you practice the suggested Techniques and as you conduct the Experiments that follow, you will quite naturally develop your own plan. Some of these Suggestions I offer you may work better for you than others. By all means, implement the workable Suggestions. Leave the Techniques that may be too difficult for you at this time to another day. At the end of this chapter you will find the necessary work pages for you to develop your personal Blueprint.

Foundational Statement

The Foundational Statement is quite important here. The Blueprint for the Spiritual Prosperity Program would require a statement of purpose. This statement may include words and phrasing that present the plan for your prosperous attainment in symbolic and emotional terms. For example: let us imagine the day-to-day life of a human, a woman or a man who is just getting by financially. This person is employed at a job that certainly does not fulfill them emotionally or artistically. The job must be kept, however, to allow the bills to be paid and paid on time.

What would a prosperous life, a life of sacred abundance, look like and feel like to this human? Let us approach this analysis from a perspective of Lessons, as we often do in this new material. Suppose that this human is learning specific Lessons regarding the ceding of power to authority figures. In this case, the person has placed their powers of Reality Creation in the hands of their employer. May we suggest that matters of self-worth enter here also? With the ceding of power to others, the self-worth is automatically diminished.

In fact, in this example, let us assume that each workday in the life of this individual is a reminder to them that they are powerless and that they face a future of continuing powerlessness. My first questions to you would be, "Where is the Soul's Intent here?" Where is the spirit of this human?" Now obviously, the spirit is not too brightly lit here. Perhaps they are too occupied with grieving over the lost life, that they do not hear the voices of spirit that call to them within their mental environment. If this person were to articulate their dilemma in a few succinct and symbolic words, they might say:

I desire to dream a dream of a satisfying occupation that brings me financial rewards beyond mere survival. Abundance!

Do you see how this human yearns for a vision of a better life, a better world for themselves? They desire a dream, perhaps because they are not experiencing pleasant, creative dreaming in their private or business lives. They do indeed require a vision, a vision from spirit, perhaps, that may inspire them and give them a sense of direction and purpose. Of course, your Foundational Statement will be concerned with your own issues and Lessons regarding prosperity. Think about these issues a few moments.

Write down your Foundational Statement here:

_____

_____

_____

_____

Now we shall present some techniques for creating Spiritual Prosperity.

Money Issues

Your money issues - your prosperity issues - are in essence <u>emotional</u> issues. Are you satisfied with your "station" in life, what you have achieved financially, materially? Your emotional responses, ongoing, to your life events, strictly determine to what degree and in what form The Abundant Universe manifests in your Personal Reality Field. Remember, recreation of your status quo reality is unconscious. In the case of money matters, your emotional subconscious responses to the events in your life are the determining factors in your continuing level of havingness. For this reason, waking up IN THE MOMENT is the prescription for achieving Spiritual Prosperity.

Technique – Consecutive Positive Assessments

Truly ALL of our exercises, techniques and experiments are designed to allow you to wake up in the moment. However, this technique of CPA we are presenting as your primary tool for this awakening. It is something that is easily learned and fun to do. The skills you acquire when practicing CPA will serve you well in your awakening on all levels of understanding.

You consecutively create each and every one of your moments in Third-Dimensional Reality. Through the creative/perceptive powers of your Inner Senses, you create and then perceive the moments of your existence. With our CPA technique, then, you will be interpreting each of your experienced moments in a positive fashion. Something good will emerge from all of your activities. You will <u>see</u> the positive wherever you look.

CPA and Lessons

Now let me explain to you this CPA from a slightly different perspective than the one I used in The Healing Regimen. Here I am asking you to address the Lesson demonstrated within each successive moment in linear time. What does that moment offer you in the way of learning? How may you experience Loving Understanding and Courage as the result of your assessment of that moment in time? This may sound difficult to accomplish, but it is merely a matter of practice until it becomes habit. You could say that what you are accomplishing here is the creation of the virtues of humankind within the moment as a result of your research INTO the moment.

CPA as Back Engineering

It may help you to think of this activity as a form of back engineering your Reality Constructs in the immediate aftermath of their creation. Let me stand upon my soapbox for just a moment (humorously)... you exist in linear time in the Third Dimension. This is the <u>appearance</u> of a reality that unfolds one moment after another. You create your own reality, and as such you have undoubtedly created BOTH prosperous moments and moments of lack. In CPA for this Spiritual Prosperity, then, you would, upon experiencing a moment of prosperous reality creation - receiving good financial news in a phone conversation, for example - contemplate the thought reality activities YOU YOURSELF used previously to create the prosperous moment. This information may come to you as an emotional tone, a feeling. You may receive an image from childhood, perhaps, a positive picture that epitomizes for you prosperity, abundance.

Again, you create your reality from ideas, images, emotions entertained within your consciousness at any one time. Within this matrix of possibilities lie the precise energies and methods for creating this prosperous moment we are describing. All of you have done this before in your lives on Earth. All of you have the potential to recreate the conditions for the experiencing of the prosperous moment, and then "remember" how you did so for future reference.

However, there may be roadblocks here that you find that "assist" you in avoiding the prosperous moment. These are the ideas and images and ruminations of your personal consciousness that have effectively kept you from the level of Prosperity Creation you desire or believe you deserve. To use our terms here: the Consciousness Units energized by these potent thoughts of lack, create Reality Constructs in the form of events, physical objects, behaviors you witness and embody that perpetuate the level of lack you are experiencing.

What do you then do in the moment, Dear Reader? I suggest you persevere, and in the following moments in the best way you can, attempt to assess your sequential moments of experiencing in positive ways, DESPITE the lapse into negative thinking. True, you may have a period of time using this technique, when you feel that it is not doing much good for you. The Abundant Universe seems quite far away. Then you continue on your own program of picking up where you left off, continually taking up the challenge to again begin the creation of the prosperous moment. You will get quite good at it over time if you take the time to practice this technique.

Technique - Distracting the ego/intellect

We have already suggested to you that you are an expert at distracting the ego/intellect from an examination of your life Lessons. Now we shall examine how you may distract your consciousness from the recreation of lack to the Divine - to a creation and perception of The Abundant Universe.

For our example here, let us say that you are currently addressing an issue of responding to financial events with fear. You may receive in your daily mail a notice that you are behind in paying a bill of some kind. As you read the stern warning, perhaps you are reminded of instances in the past when you failed to meet your financial obligations and were punished in some way. Because these negative memories are so rich in emotional intensity, you may be swept away for a few moments as you literally travel to that moment in time to experience the negative fear-producing emotions. This is a simple example of Astral Travel. You have been triggered by the receipt of the bill to go back in time for a re-experiencing of what we might term "financial worry."

Now let us devise a response to receiving the bill that will assist in the creation of positive realities rather than the continuation of negatives. The trick here is to awaken in the moment so that you may have conscious control IN the current moment. Thus you would possibly open the bill, read the stern warning, and before your subconscious can take you back in time for a reliving of the negative states of financial worry, you exert awareness of your current Moment Point. When you are established in the moment, at the second of recognition of the negative, fear-producing material, you imagine a positive outcome. This is best done by remembering positive outcomes of the past. Using your Intention, you distract your ego/intellect from responding unconsciously to the fear-producing material.

The negative historical data can be quite persuasive, so you must persevere in this moment. You might remind yourself that you are existing in tandem with the Divine - with All That Is - and that there is an incoming message to be received. Then you would imagine with full sensory awareness your receiving sums of money, for instance, enabling you to meet your financial obligations.

This imaginative construct exists in your current moment, therefore, and in your future also as it is manifest enabling you to pay your bill, yet it is based on a positive financial event that occurred in your past. It may be advantageous for you to "mine" your perceived past for these positive financial experiences, no matter how small or insignificant they may at first appear. The emotional tone is what is important here. The idea of the Divine, prosperity and The Abundant Universe are the most important features.

The feeling of contentment and abundance you felt when your caregiver gave you a quarter to buy some candy when you were a child becomes an important reference point for you in these experiments. You are recreating these positive feelings of hope, faith etc. IN THE CURRENT MOMENT. You will then "push" the positive moments into the future as you embody the positive state of consciousness - abundance - moment-to-moment. This is easily done. And I specifically suggest you turn to your childhood experiences for the positive states of consciousness, for it was as a child that you most probably first experienced using your powerful imagination to create those things you desired.

Technique - Giving it All Away

My friend Mark here is quite concerned - troubled (humorously) - by my assertion that to be truly successful and to truly perceive and create The Abundant Universe, the student must, in the final analysis, "give it all away." To be sure, at first glance, this statement seems to imply that you will lose everything that you have worked for in the Spiritual Prosperity Program. Certainly, if you give your wealth or material possessions to others, you no longer have possession of them. You are without them. How does one put food on the table or pay the bills if what is received is continually given away to others - individuals and collectives. These are earnest and excellent questions to ask. In answering them, please allow me to pass on to you, Dear Reader, another fact of life for you in physical existence.

Now others before me have stated this bluntly, so this is certainly not something that you do not already know. **You receive what you transmit**. In terms of energy - Light energy, which is, as we have stated earlier, the "stuff" of all created realities - you get what you give. There is a popular aphorism that applies here, "What goes around come around." The statement implies, I believe, that there is a type of karmic balancing dynamic that occurs within the lives of humans. My readers know my feelings on karma and the Eastern theory of Reality Creation. I believe it is quite correct to a degree, but perhaps it should be taken to "the nth degree." Let me explain... you live your lives all at once, within the spacious moment, the eternal moment that exists NOW. Your lives are certainly not sequential, for there is no such thing as linear time in the experiencing of the Soul, your true reality.

Now as you are within this Moment Point possibly sensing your connection to your many lives past, present and future, you are receiving energy from these lives and you are also transmitting energy to these lives. Additionally, at this moment, let us say that you are also receiving energy from and transmitting energy to COUNTLESS humans within your Consensus Reality. You are also NOW quite naturally transmitting energy to and receiving energy from the many elemental forms within your Personal Reality.

What does this Light energy have to do with The Abundant Universe and giving it all away? Let us go back to my earlier discussions of CUs. Greatly simplified, this Light energy is the medium for the Reality Creation project. Let us say that Light holds within it the potencies and potentialities of <u>all</u> of our essential metaphors in our theory of Reality Creation. Now you may remember that the CUs are electromagnetic. As they assemble into Gestalts of Consciousness, they do so according to energies of attraction and repulsion: like with like, yet opposites assemble within the whole as counterparts to their opposites, and so on. **This is the organizing principle of life.** I have already described to you how All That Is - essentially Love in action - creates realities that are not Love, that are the opposites indeed of Love. In this way Reality Creation evolves, differentiates along every conceivable avenue of development. It is just this way with Light, my friend; the Love Light of All That Is.

Transmitter of Love

Here then is the secret. You will receive what you transmit, for you will be a transmitter of Love. The student attaches Love and positive emotion energy to all thoughtforms that are transmitted within their mental environment. In mundane matters of daily living, then, while you pay your bills, you are attaching Love to them with your thoughts. While you work at your job, you are sending out thoughtforms of Love to your colleagues and to your customers. While you interact with your family and friends, you are sending thoughtforms of Love into their mental environments. You are intentionally sending out these thoughtforms of Love to all concerned with no expectation of receiving <u>anything</u> in return. This is a form of giving it all away, is it not?

As you are also, as a researcher, a student of your own self-development, interpreting each of your experienced moments in positive Loving ways - as best you can, of course, perhaps you have not yet achieved perfection in this technique (humorously) - you will be contributing to the experiencing of positive realities with this divine perspective.

The mental construct, the thought-energy hologram we are calling Giving It All Away, is based in Love and Courage. With every transmission - for example, donating to your causes - you attach the holographic Idea Construct. This attachment powers the thoughtform on the subtle levels. As my Holographic Inserts to you in the Third Dimension serve to enlighten and inform you, in the same way, your transmission of these thoughtforms attached to your mundane behaviors may serve to enlighten, empower and PROSPER the recipients. It is all energy, once again. It is all Light energy in the form of the Consciousness Units.

True Giving

As I suggested in my first book since my return, your practice of giving to worthy causes only when you may claim a deduction from your taxes, is not at all Giving in its truest sense. This is not the magical act of Giving that we are teaching you in this new material. To be honest, it is a sad form of money exchange, this corporate giving that is celebrated in your world. Many of you who give in this fashion expect something in return. Whether it is a tax deduction, God's grace or simply the good karma that is so valued by the modern human, something is expected in return for the giving. Might I state it bluntly here? You taint this process with your bargaining. In Giving there are only the communication streams of Beings of Light. There is only the transformation of Light into something else. There is no bargaining.

I believe it might help you to think of your Giving of your money, your time, your Loving Understanding to others is simply the transformation of your Light Energy into what is needed by the recipient of the Giving. From this perspective, you may envision the immediate transformation of your gift of Light into what is desired, what is required by the receiver. In this context, the recipient uses their Reality Creation energies to collaborate with you on the subtle levels in the co-creation of the necessary constructs.

Take for example here my previous description of the children in your poor undeveloped countries. I am not suggesting that you refuse the tax deduction you "deserve" for contributing to their cause - though that would indeed demonstrate your commitment to true Giving - but please try attaching your powerful Light energies to the gift when you do make your donations for the purchase of food, medical care, and so on. And remember, Dear Reader, there is no pity here in this true reality of the Soul. You are equals on the subtle levels, equals who are merely learning different Lessons. Do not give because you feel sorry for the other; give because you acknowledge the opportunity to endorse the Courage of another.

It may help you to think of yourself as a Light Body in this exercise. I am a Being of Light. You are a Being of Light. On the etheric levels, within the Telepathic Network, we both have equal powers. We communicate with one another instantaneously. We observe the instantaneous manifestation of our thoughtforms. You are in the Third Dimension and you have a perception of a lag-time in manifestation. However, this is merely a perception. Your reality is my reality at its base. Your holographic messages are received INSTANTLY by the recipient. On the etheric plane, the recipient IMMEDIATELY benefits from your Loving and Courageous act of imbuing your transmissions with these creative energies.

Now if you are coming from a perception of lack, it is quite true that on the physical reality level, it appears that you are giving up your resources, your money, your personal property. However, as I said, the Soul Self of each of you engaged in the interaction knows quite definitely that this is not the case. As the Soul Self of the cashier at the market, for example, receives the energy from your transmission as you hand them your payment for your food products, your

Higher Self receives an influx of beneficial energy from them. Now on the physical plane, all that you may notice is a slight knowing smile on the face of the cashier. This is your cue, however, that your thoughtform is manifesting.

Voting with the Pocketbook

Here Mark is protesting somewhat that it is a far stretch of the imagination to believe that a benign Loving transmission sent to the Soul Self of a bank owner would have such a positive effect. Do you see how this thought reveals Mark's beliefs regarding banks and "the rich?" I would suggest that when Mark "heals" this belief regarding wealth and abundance, he may begin to enjoy more glimpses of The Abundant Universe. (humorously)

Let me digress on this point... it is ALL Love, Dear Reader. Even the millionaire banker, then, is created from Love. Yet let us just say for the sake of argument, that the banker is a war profiteer. Through supporting armament manufacturers or the military, this banker prospers from death, hatred, war. "What good," you might ask, "does my Loving construct do in this context?" I have suggested in our last two books, that you might "vote with your pocketbook," by selecting the most appropriate, Loving and peaceful institutions with which to do business, and then doing business with these institutions. In this way, you are supporting, on both the physical and the metaphysical levels, the fulfillment of positive values. This takes research, of course. This activity may be thought of as the assessment of the Personal Reality Field with regards to the financial or business aspects of your life. Where will you put the Loving and Courageous energies of your being? From what institutions will you withhold your creative energies? Again, this is all about allying with select Gestalts of Consciousness, Entities, Beings of Light. This is conscious co-creation.

Technique - Suspending Disbelief

The technique of suspending disbelief will assist you in creating further moments of prosperity after you are successful in creating a "glimpse" of The Abundant Universe. For example: suppose you have completed your investigative work, you have gone within to examine your personal conceptualization of The Abundant Universe. *(See experiment this chapter. mf)* Your idea of abundance, for the time being, might involve, perhaps, receiving an unexpected windfall, a sum of money, several hundred dollars let us say, in the mails. Now you have done your work here. You have attached Love to all of your thoughtforms. You have magically anticipated this gift and now you are witnessing the manifestation.

At the moment of realization, when you connect the windfall to your Spiritual Prosperity behaviors and thoughts, depending on your "issues" - self-image, experiencing of Negative Emotions - you may find it difficult or quite easy TO ACCEPT RESPONSIBILITY for this creative work. If you have doubts and ascribe the gift to coincidence, you diminish your power in that moment. However, if you confidently express your gratitude, Loving Understanding and Courage in that moment, you are adding to your powers of manifestation. You are suspending disbelief - the negative assessment of the act of manifestation - for just the moment. Then you would successively suspend disbelief in your growing powers, moment-to-moment in the "future."

Suspending disbelief is a form of silencing the internal censor - that aspect of your consciousness that wishes to keep you entranced in the creation of status quo realities. Over time, this voice will be replaced by the encouraging messages from Beings of Light - your Guides who seek to assist you in expanding your awareness.

The Metaphorical Tools

Of course you may use all of the Metaphorical Tools we have described in our new books. An important addition you might consider is the creation of The Well of Good Fortune, or some other potent metaphor tailored to your own sensitivities. Here the object is to call upon your symbols of wealth, good fortune, havingness, and combine them into one powerful image, phrase, song, object or what have you. Give this Metaphorical Tool a fitting name. Empower it with your thoughts and your limitless energies. In my example, you might empower with your energies a visualized well, perhaps somewhere in a beautiful forest. Within this well is the abundance and good fortune you desire. Going to The Well of Good Fortune, then, might be a simple matter of imagining yourself entering a forest, observing The Well, and visualizing the desired Reality Constructs coming up and out of the well, perhaps as you turn the crank. The Metaphorical Tools are easy to create. They are most effective when you can feed them your divine energy. Personalize these tools and make them your own.

The Radio Dial Metaphor may also be ably used in Spiritual Prosperity. Just as you perhaps used this tool to tune-in the healing elements and tune-out the disease-producing GOCs in The Healing Regimen, here you may use your Radio Dial to tune-in on the impulses from your Simultaneous Lives, for example, that seek to direct your vision toward The Abundant Universe. You would then, at the same time, tune-out the impulses and influences from Negative Entities, other existences that are experiencing lack and those Negative Emotions that hamper your attainment of Spiritual Prosperity.

Now for some experimentation in Spiritual Prosperity.

Experiment - Perceiving/creating The Abundant Universe
Hypothesis: you may tune-in the abundant universe

Perception creates reality in the Third Dimension. When you visualize and embody The Abundant Universe, you are CREATING and SUSTAINING this GOC. You are withdrawing from this template of creation, the highly personalized elements in the form of CUs that you require to create the reality of abundance within your Personal Reality Field. You can't help yourself, you see. Your thoughts are composed of CUs. All Consciousness seeks manifestation of <u>itself</u>. By simply thinking of something you lend your efforts towards creating it.

Now you each have your idealized view of the <u>perfect</u> world. You know quite well what objects, what types of people, and what behaviors would exist in this world. For your own reasons, however, you choose not to put your energies towards manifesting The Abundant Universe. As I have said to you, your "reasons" for doing something or not doing something in your life - the denials, the intellectualizations - serve to aid you in encountering and experiencing your Lessons.

For example: consider a human that finds themselves within a precarious financial situation. All is lost financially for whatever reasons in physical reality. Additionally, this human makes matters worse by continually blaming themselves for the financial loss. It is a personal issue. They feel as though they have failed personally as well as financially.

Now this negative assessment of the Personal Reality, as you may remember, serves to perpetuate it. The person is tying all of the domains of existence into one knot. They are in effect saying, "I have failed financially because I am a failure personally. I am a bad person, an undeserving person." The entire existence is colored with this negative assessment.

How does this person perceive and create The Abundant Universe under these drastic conditions?

Remember, this is an unconscious process. If you wish to explore this GOC that is your personalized Abundant Universe, then you must go to the unconscious and explore. It would be wise to use the emotionally neutral state of Trance. In the Trance State the subject may gain a broader view of the life and the conditions of existence. The agenda of negative Reality Creation is easily interrupted by the Trance. The opportunity for introducing changes into the reality creation strategies is made available.

Perform your Ritual of Sanctuary

Attain your Trance State. If you are in your quiet meditation area, relax your body, breathe deeply, rest upon the floor or do whatever behaviors assist you in creating the Trance. If you are out in the world, you may, as we have suggested in the last book, tie the attainment of the Trance State to a gesture such as snapping the fingers, rubbing a good-luck piece or whatever suits you.

In this experiment we will assist the researcher in withdrawing from the negative reality of lack and "waking up" in The Abundant Universe. This has a distinctly magical quality to it.

As you are resting comfortably, out in the world or in your meditation area in your home, within your Trance State, embody the perception of entering the GOC we are calling The Abundant Universe in this manuscript. A playful approach here may be best. As a child would, imagine yourself in your inner world, coming into a kingdom, perhaps, in which all of the desired Reality

173

Constructs that populate your personalized Abundant Universe are displayed. You are venturing out and away from your normal world to visit this inner world where the outer world is created.

As we have suggested in our other experiments in using the Trance State, the information stream may be sensed in various ways. The GOC may present itself to you "full blown" as in an intense, multisensory visionary experience. Or you may get your "glimpse" of this idealized state as though you were receiving a Holographic Insert or other inspirational missive from the nonphysical world. You may hear sounds and voices that represent abundance and good fortune for you personally. You may also simply experience a "good feeling," a pervasive sensation of grace, a feeling that all is well with you in your world.

As you receive your data, note the information for documenting later, then proceed to go deeper into your relaxed state and uncover more Findings. Typically, because the emotions experienced in perceiving The Abundant Universe are so positive, you will be motivated to continue your explorations. When you feel as though you have enough information from the session, return to full sensory awareness of Third-Dimensional Reality, bringing with you The Abundant Universe that you have perceived/created into existence on the subtle levels. If you are out and about, on a park bench let us say, snap your fingers, rub your good-luck piece. If you are indoors in your meditation area, give yourself the suggestion that you will return to your normal awareness with the full memories of The Abundant Universe intact.

Findings - Document your findings.

Experiment - Collaborating with Soul Family Members

Hypothesis: you may manage soul family relationships in the trance state.

We have stated before in these new manuscripts, that each and every human being that you meet - including the delivery person and the teller at the local bank - is in your life at that moment to teach you something. Many of the more intense relationships you create with these humans are Soul Family connections. Of this broad group of Soul Family members is included a group of humans who are within your field of experiencing to interact with you in the learning of Lessons regarding the acquisition of money and the perception of The Abundant Universe.

This statement may bring to mind events from your own life in which you were quite intrigued with the good fortune that came your way, at the hands of one of these mysterious extended family members. Or perhaps you were "taken for a ride" by one of your acquaintances, and relieved of some of your hard-earned money. Either way, you were learning Lessons from Soul Family members. These inter-actions often have an element of Fate attached to them, as though they were "meant to be," to coin a phrase from your New Agers. However, as you know, you and your colleagues are making it happen. You are just currently unaware of the intricacies of this cooperative effort.

The perspective of experiencing Lessons from within a broad collective called the Soul Family can be learned. I suggest you conduct the following experi-ment with the idea that you are <u>already</u> embodying this perspective.

Perform your Ritual of Sanctuary

The first step here would be to identify those Soul Family members who may act as partners in the re-alization of the abundance you require. Using your Inner Senses you may home-in on these personali-ties in your times of meditation. Some you may have already identified within your field of experiencing as potential allies. This is a form of communicating with the Energy Personality of another. *(See Experi-ment Chapter Ten. mf)* You will be identifying specific characteristics of personality and Soul that will assist you in creating good fortune within the lives of all of you. Everyone benefits, you see.

Now this group may be small in number or it may be quite large. Either way, you will be working with these humans on the subtle levels. You might think of yourself as the business manager of this assembly, and you are working with their Higher Selves for mutually beneficial purposes. This is your Intent. You are grounded in your sense of Divine Will to communicate your interests to these humans via their Spirit Guides - their Energy Personalities. If the EP of the Soul Family member resists, do not press it further. You are not to force yourself on others in any way. This is a sacred form of communication. If you meet with resistance, move on to another potential partner.

In the mundane world, there may be no signs that you are interacting with these people in any special fashion. "Business as usual," as you say. However, do note the attainment of group goals that could have never been realized had these secret connections not been made. **Findings** - Document the establishment of connections with Soul Family members and the realization of Soul Family goals in matters of abundance.

Experiment - Calling In Your Guides
Hypothesis: the nonphysical beings may assist you in the spiritual prosperity program.

Can you see that you are pursuing these studies for a purpose? You are well into this description of the Spiritual Prosperity Program. I believe it is safe to say that you are concerned about the level of prosperity that you are currently experiencing. In other words, in the nomenclature of this Teaching, one of your Lessons for your current existence might well be to investigate the possibilities for increasing abundance in your life.

Now you may have been drawn to this new book of mine for a variety of reasons. But can you accept the possibility that perhaps the main reason is that you were "prompted" from within to look at the new Seth books? If you can accept this premise, then perhaps you may take it one step further, and admit the possibility that you are already in touch with nonphysical beings.

Inner promptings are often communications from nonphysical beings. Whether you believe that it was I Seth who has prompted you, or your own Spirit Guide, or simply your individual human consciousness - the amalgam of "conversations" between you and your Reincarnational Existences - do you see that you are possibly already quite well along on your path of belief change? Many of the exercises, experiments and techniques in the new material are for the express purpose of belief change in the reader. Your belief in a nonphysical reality populated by Beings of Light and other Gestalts of Consciousness is a prerequisite for your continued growth as a Soul.

There are specific nonphysical beings available within your mental environment that may be enlisted in the achievement of Spiritual Prosperity. You may refer to these Light Bodies as Prosperity Guides, if you wish. They are specially gifted beings that have served as financial advisors to humanity. Mark has recently contacted a group of these Guides that goes by the name of the Crystal Light Messengers. They exist just outside of your Earthly realm as Fifth-Dimensional Beings. Simply have the Intent that you will contact your Prosperity Guides while in your times of meditation within your sacred state of Sanctuary. Then you will meet with success.

The researcher may also use the Energy Personality and other Helpers in this program. Now this is assuming you have already made these connections. If you have not, please simply "pretend" that you have made these connections and then conduct the following experiment.

Perform your Ritual of Sanctuary

Relax your body. Attain your Trance State. Here we are "opening the gates," you might say, to your divine consciousness. Now you are protected; you are in your state of Sanctuary. As you open the gates you are doing so with the security that comes with divine protection. The Negative Emotions have no place here. Only the Divine is made manifest under these conditions. So perhaps using this metaphor of an opening gate or other portal, visualize your assistants in attaining prosperity and abundance crossing the threshold and coming into your awareness.

The nonphysical beings of whatever stripe and purpose, emit Light according to the conditions of their particular existences. Vibration, you see, is their calling card. It is with your Inner Senses, also, that you may distinguish one Guide from another, procure their names, ask what services they offer, and so on. Use your Inner Senses in the best way that suits you for this purpose.

This experiment may take just a few minutes. As we have stated elsewhere, your Guides are literally on the threshold of your awareness, waiting to be acknowledged. Now some of my readers are perhaps unaware of how easily this is done. They are expecting something difficult to accomplish. They are therefore quite surprised when they encounter one or more of these divine Guides on just the most cursory of exploratory voyages. So I suggest to you that you approach this experiment as one that is easily done. Here you are a child, you see, having some fun with your imagination. When you are done having fun with your nonphysical associates, give yourself the suggestion to return to full sensory awareness in Third-Dimensional Reality.

Findings - Document the names of your Guides and the services they offer.

Experiment - Reading The Emotional Body
Hypothesis: the emotional body displays the causes
and remedies of lack.

In this experiment you will use your Inner Sense
of sight, your Auric Vision, to perceive the emotional
elements within your consciousness that prevent you
from experiencing The Abundant Universe. This vision
of your emotional issues relative to prosperity may
take the form of a dramatic vignette displayed for you
as you close your eyes to relax. Within this dramatic
presentation you may witness, for example, a replay
of an event from your perceived past, in which you
experienced disempowerment in some form. Perhaps
you were robbed by a bully when you were a child.
Perhaps an adult had suggested to you that you would
never be successful in your life, that you were "not
good with money" or "irresponsible." The communication stream from your inner world may take the form
of a narrative, perhaps a rumination of a series of
words or sentences. The focus here is on "causes" of
present lack in your reality, and so you may remember words and phrases that portray you as, in some
way, incompetent or unable to ever succeed. You may
have a sudden feeling of distaste, or fear, or other
Negative Emotion that acts as a catalyst, allowing you
to go deeper in your exploration to the roots of your
current less-than-satisfactory life condition. As in your

previous investigations in this Research Project, the vision may have elements other than sight, i.e. smell, taste, hearing. And again, please be prepared to face some difficult material - ideas and images you may have kept undercover for many years.

Perform your Ritual of Sanctuary

Relax your physical body in the way that most pleases you. Close your eyes and breathe deeply for a few moments. Remember that the vision of the emotional issues may be perceived as existing within the torso of your body, within the heart region. The focus here is on causes, most probably from your past, of present financial insecurity. These are emotional injuries sustained during difficult Lessons learned usually in childhood in your current and your other lives. In your current life, these Negative Emotions have sustained themselves over time, preventing you from experiencing The Abundant Universe that is your birthright.

You may re-experience a specific event that occurred in your perceived past that represented a break from your innocent childhood experiencing and marked a new trajectory of development for you as a maturing "socialized" human. Perhaps you may view that point where you gave up some of your Reality Creation energies to authority figures: parent, teacher, relative. The feeling tone of your experiences will help you to determine where to go with this experiment. Ask for direction from your Guides. Use your Inner Senses as a compass. Your Intuition will guide you if you are clear and persistent.

Findings - Immediately document in some way your experiences with reading The Emotional Body.

Experiment - Belief Revision

Hypothesis: beliefs that support lack may be altered to support prosperity.

Your beliefs have created the precise level of lack that you are experiencing. Your existence is a direct result of your Reality Creation activities according to beliefs that you hold. Any example of poverty or lack within your Personal Reality, therefore, can be traced back to a specific Idea Construct that you perceive as being quite true. In The Healing Regimen we presented an experiment in belief adaptation. In this new regimen we will present a similar experiment with a different focus.

Perform Your Ritual of Sanctuary

Assume your Trance State through your preferred method. Now you are relaxed. Now you are focused on searching for "causes" within your mental environment for the lack you are experiencing. These causes are your beliefs, however you may wish to visualize this concept. What does a belief represent to you, in so far as symbols, feelings, sensations of various types are concerned? Again, it is often the case that the first thing that comes to mind may hold the most information. Your Inner Self is attempting to tell you something, you see, to reveal something of value to you. The information may be quite complex in construction, as in a profound revelation - an epiphany - or quite simple, as in a fleeting emotion of some kind.

For example: suppose that your first thought within the Trance State was the statement, "This is not going to work," and what if this statement operates as a powerful loop - a rumination - within your consciousness. If this were the case, do you see how difficult it might be for you to approach these studies and experimentation and be successful to any degree? Now this is an extremely common first discovery for the explorer of nonphysical reality. This simple Idea Construct is quite powerful in its simplicity, when it is looped, you see, when it is repeated incessantly within the mental environment. It has the power to adversely affect the Reality Creation activities on all levels, not merely the financial.

Now what if you were to revise the phrase somewhat: "This <u>may</u> work." Now there is hope. Now there is the opportunity for change. Here in this experiment, using your Intent, what we are referring to as Divine Will, you alter the negative rumination - the substance of negative belief - to make room for hope and opportunity. "This <u>may</u> work. This Spiritual Prosperity Program may work." This is a positive rumination that may assist you in the creation of positive realities. As you witness your improving reality, your beliefs about what is possible are changed. You are opening up. You are accepting the possibility of positive change in your world.

Findings - Note your discoveries in Belief Revision.

Experiment - Prosperity Talk

Hypothesis: positive suggestions help to create prosperous realities.

As you may now be well advanced in your achieving of the Trance State, through participating in the exercises in this book, we will simply present this experiment as one of self-conditioning or self-hypnosis through reading affirmative statements or listening to recorded positive suggestions while in Trance. As we have discussed earlier in this manuscript, your beliefs and their emotional underpinnings may be more readily accessible than you might think. After all, your beliefs are busy <u>nonstop</u> creating (on a subconscious level) your perceived reality. With the approach that this is not hard to do, it is possible to expect the Idea Constructs supporting your beliefs to be there in your mental environment, observable indeed, without attending years of therapy. (humorously)

Perform your Ritual of Sanctuary

The preliminary work entails an exploration of the consciousness, seeking out those thoughts, images and emotional content that support the beliefs. Enter a

185

light state of Trance and with pen and paper or through talking into a recorder, you might spontaneously have a discussion with yourself on what are the problematic beliefs. Document what first comes to your mind and go from there. There is an underlying assumption here that your Inner Self is primed to reveal this information to you. Your Soul Self is well aware of this voyage of yours and is undoubtedly waiting to assist you. Simply take down what this aspect of your consciousness is trying to tell you. Document without censoring. You may analyze later.

Come back to full sensory awareness.

After this initial stage of information gathering is complete, consider the opposites of the problematic beliefs or a positive adaptation of the beliefs and write them down or record these suggestions for playback. Enter your Trance State again and either read the suggestions to yourself or listen to the playback on your recorder.

For example: in your belief work you may have discovered that you have a circular inner comment that is consistently voicing the opinion of someone from your past: "You are stupid. You will never succeed." Using our technique of revising this unfortunate comment - a comment perhaps made in the heat of the moment without any true conviction behind it, you see - we might create the following: "You have a strong natural intelligence. A successful life awaits you." You could then inscribe several different permutations of this message on a paper to read while in a light Trance. Or you could read the various suggestions into your recorder for playback while in a deeper Trance. The object here, which may seem obvious to you now, is to instill the positive suggestions into the mental awareness over time, until the historical comment is supplanted by the improved positive suggestions.

Findings - Document in some form your belief work and your attempts to supplant problematic beliefs with positive suggestions.

Experiment - Consulting Your Prosperous Selves
Hypothesis: you can receive advice from your future and probable selves.

Let us assume that you are currently experiencing lack in some area of your life. Now the idea of lack is tied to a veritable field of multidimensional negative experiencing. Not only are you experiencing lack in your current Reincarnational Existence, then, but you are also adding to the experience of lack within your other Simultaneous Lives. Remember that you are connected to these other lives so that each of the personalities experiencing these lives will sense your lack, your feelings of disempowerment, monetary peril etc. within their mental environment, as you sense their negative states of consciousness within yours.

Fortunately, within your Simultaneous Lives, including your probable existences, there are also those who are experiencing the <u>opposite</u> of lack - abundance. You shall attempt to contact these lives in your meditations in order to gather information on how you may also create abundance within your own current life. It is a form of sharing within a family, in a manner of speaking, a family of consciousness. And just as you might in your current existence ask for and receive advice from an uncle or cousin on how to invest your money wisely, you may inquire on the subtle levels what your other lives are doing to create abundance.

If you have been with us in these books of ours, trying out some of the exercises and at least attempting some of the experiments, by now you will have gained some glimpses into the unknown reality - the world inhabited by your multidimensional counterparts throughout space and time. For you this experiment may reveal information that will quicken your journey, as you look to expand your vistas of perception. If you are just joining us in these esoteric pursuits, this experiment may strike you as rather preposterous, entirely too farfetched to even consider attempting. I urge you to make the effort in spite of your doubt, in spite of your inexperience. You may be pleasantly surprised.

Perform your Ritual of Sanctuary

Relax your body and enter a fairly deep Trance State. The object in this experiment is to seek contact with your Simultaneous Lives and probable existences that are experiencing abundance. With this goal as the focus of your Intent - your Divine Will - simply reflect on these words as you go deeper and deeper in your meditation. Now you are guided by your Intent here. The consciousness will naturally make those changes necessary to allow contact with the Souls experiencing abundance. It may be best not to force the issue. Trying too hard - attempting to direct the flow of energy - may be counterproductive. Let the mind wander, in other words. Remember, there is an assumption in these investigations that you are being watched over by nonphysical beings. You will be guided to your destination if you will only "go with the flow" of consciousness.

You know what an abundant feeling "feels like." As you perceive with your Inner Senses the mental environments of your lives as they express these positive emotions, go towards these emotional expressions. Feelings of Courage and Loving Understanding may arise here. Confidence and self-assurance may be readily discernible. If you are sensing these emotional tones, you may be assured that you are on the right track. If you wish to go further with this exploration, ask for names and dates of these other lives. Go as far as you wish in your investigations seeking "proof" that you are making these connections. Return to full sensory awareness when you sense that you are done.

The information you requested in Trance may come to you in the form of impulses, as you go about your waking reality, just as we have suggested in our previous volume in this series. Might I suggest that the emotional tones that "carry" these impulses into your awareness are of the abundant, prosperous variety? (humorously) That is how you will be able to identify their origin. As always, use your free will to either ignore or act on these impulses.

Findings - Document impulses you have received from your other lives as a result of these inquiries.

Experiment - Gambling with the Guides
Hypothesis: you may use the advice of your guides in games of chance.

With regards to availing yourself of the assistance of your Guides in matters of prosperity, monetary increase and the like, I must present to you this fact of existence: although you may certainly ask your guides for "divine guidance" as to what are the winning lottery numbers, or what are the winning machines at the casino, and so on, you still remain within the matrix of probabilities in your Reality Creation activities. This matrix includes the casino itself, if I may use this example, and everything in the casino.

Now let us use an example in a particular form of gambling here, to further this disclaimer from Seth. (humorously) In this example, the subject is accessing their Guides while they are engaged in placing bets on the numbers of a roulette wheel game in a normal casino somewhere, in one of your gambling capitals in the U.S.A., in Europe or elsewhere. Let us say that the Guides are doing their best in assisting the student's experiment in prosperity-creation and they are presenting possible winning numbers into the mental environment of the student telepathically.

As you know, there are innumerable probable permutations of events possible within each successive moment of the existence of this theoretical student. Additionally, the outcome of any roll of the dice or spin of the ball in these matters is not truly known and identified in "bedrock reality," as you say, until the very last microsecond of the activity of the dice, the ball or the card in any particular instance. The outcome of any gambling event, then, is a cooperative effort between the Consciousness Units that compose every human, every machine, every cubic foot of space, every piece of furniture within that casino.

Also, it is important to remember that each of you in physical reality, in whatever Reality Creation activities you are involved, are doing so for the learning of particular Lessons. Your Guides are not allowed to present information to you that would interfere with the learning of these Lessons. Let me say that if you are to attempt these experiments in Prosperity Creation, that you first examine your issues with regards to prosperity - the monetary Lessons that you are to learn while in your current body in your current timeframe.

Now if you are to conduct your Prosperity Creation experiments in the field, you will have previously committed the particulars of this experiment to memory. You will also have done your belief work and your "homework" regarding Lessons for this lifetime concerning abundance. Because you will be out in the world conducting your research, it will be necessary to have perfected conducting the Ritual of Sanctuary and the creation of the Trance State while in public.

This experiment is concerned with prophecy. You shall be predicting the momentary activities of the elements in a game of chance. Let us assume you are in a public setting somewhere, engaged in this game.

Perform your Ritual of Sanctuary

Enter your relaxed state and enter your Trance State. Now conduct your experiment of calling in your Guides. All of these preparatory activities can be an internal process for you, without any outward signs. As in our other experiments, it may be wise to assume the playful attitude of a child in these endeavors. An overly-serious attitude may short-circuit the intuitive processes.

Now call upon your Inner Senses, if entirely appropriate, to reveal that information you may require to "win." To accomplish this, you might project your Auric Vision out onto the gaming table and allow your Inner Senses to create a visual representation of the winning numbers, cards, and so on. If you are oriented to sound, perhaps you could ask your Guides to whisper to you the information required. Whatever sensory input you are comfortable with, arrange for your Prosperity Guides and perhaps your Energy Personality to feed to you this information at the appropriate times.

The researcher may expect varying levels of good fortune - positive Reality Creation - to be made manifest in this experiment. You are challenging the "laws" of chance. Any wins beyond these laws, therefore, are an indication that you are on the right track. When you are successful, remember the state of consciousness you embodied immediately prior to the win and reproduce that state as best you can toward future wins. This game of chance is indeed a game. Have fun with it, just as I have suggested you have fun also in the creation of your life in the other domains.

Findings - Remember for future reference the feeling tones and states of consciousness that signal a winning game.

The Blueprint

consists of the studious application of the Rituals of Prosperity, the Techniques and your personal Findings to the issue at hand.

CPA	Consecutive Positive Assessments
DTEI	Distracting the Ego/Intellect
GIAA	Giving it All Away
SD	Suspending Disbelief
MT	Metaphorical Tools
PCTAA	Perceiving/Creating the Abundant Universe
CWSFM	Collaborating with Soul Family Members
CIYG	Calling in your Guides
RTEB	Reading The Emotional Body
BR	Belief Revision
PT	Prosperity Talk
CYPS	Consulting your Prosperous Selves
TOL	Transmitter of Love
VWTP	Voting with the Pocketbook
GWTG	Gambling with the Guides

7 DAY CALENDAR

At the end of the day, assess on a scale of 1 to 7 your use of the Rituals and Techniques suggested in the Spiritual Prosperity Program.

1 - Very little Use   2 - Some Use 3 - Moderate Use   4 - Regular Use
5 - Consistent Use   6 - Concerted Use   7 - Very focussed Use

	M	T	W	T	F	S	S
CPA							
DTEI							
GIAA							
SD							
MT							
PCTAA							
CWSFM							
CIYG							
RTEB							
BR							
PT							
CYPS							
TOL							
VWTP							
GWTG							

CHAPTER EIGHT

Wisdom Lessons

Dialogue - Harsh Conditions
7/7/05 6:00 AM

Seth: *Do you see how this chapter may bring hope to some of our readers?*

Mark: *Yes I do. It certainly explains why some people seem to thrive and prosper within very challenging "negative" conditions.*

Seth: *Exactly. We are reminding these readers - those that are experiencing these harsh conditions - that they have chosen these lives. Also, we are reminding them that they may be on the end of their incarnational trajectories, and may be headed for the higher realms. This may be a good motivation for some to begin using our techniques to transform the negativity they are experiencing into Courage and Loving Understanding. This Soul work is necessary before one may progress to the higher-dimensional realms.*

Lessons of Negativity

In this chapter we shall hopefully provide you with the opportunity to address the most pressing and important Lessons for you in your current existence. Now truly ALL of your Lessons are "wisdom" Lessons, in that you experience Soul Evolution when you are engaged in learning these Lessons. So that the gaining of prosperity within a life of perceived lack and poverty, may be considered the gaining of wisdom, as well as the facing of perceived extremely difficult, traumatic material from your past may be considered the gaining of wisdom. However, in this material we will attempt to provide you with the motivation you require to do what you must do in facing your most difficult Lessons - the Lessons of Negativity, pain and suffering.

For I trust you would agree that the positive Lessons - of Love, of experiencing prosperity, of developing friendships - need much less motivation for the average human to engage in and "do the homework" required, than do the Lessons of Negativity. The Lessons of Love will take care of themselves over time. Whereas with the Lessons of Negativity, the primary reason you have not yet learned these Lessons is that you are indeed avoiding them.

Facing the Music

The Lessons of Negativity can be faced now. You have the tools to deal with these Lessons. Now this is the way that it works for you with all types of behaviors: whatever elicits the perception of satisfaction or happiness is pursued relentlessly. Whatever <u>seems</u> to create the Negative Emotions is most usually avoided. There are, of course, exceptions to this rule in every life. We have noted previously in this material the tendency for the "depressed" person to create Reality Constructs that perpetuate the state of depression, as though there were a certain muted satisfaction in depression. Generally, however, the negative states are avoided by most of you.

For example: this is particularly true in the developed nations as you call yourselves. You are certainly "developed" in so far as access to material wealth is concerned. However, it is the rest of the world's peoples who have the edge in matters of spiritual understanding, spiritual wealth. In the developed countries you are easily diverted from spiritual considerations by the many objects of mass consumption made available to you through your shopping centers, for example, through your mass media, and so on. You, Dear Reader, are easily diverted in the moment by these requests from your creators of "shiny things." You are easily distracted for you are "waiting for an excuse" to avoid your Lessons. As we have suggested in these books, like children, many of you would rather not consider your Lessons in physical reality, and would rather buy something you desire to feel good for that moment. If you are feeling anxious or depressed, you buy something. If you are grieving or in physical or psychological pain, you buy something to "make yourself feel better."

As you know, it is the adrenaline and other substances released in your body that creates this "feeling better" state of consciousness. Over time you become dependent on this satisfied emotional state and you may find yourself purchasing more than you need or can afford to keep "happy." The Lessons of Negativity are thus avoided.

Two-Step Activity

This is how your Third-Dimensional system was "set up." It is an arena for the experiencing of Negative Emotions. However, eventually you must face this aspect of your personality. You each are called upon to address the negative thoughts within your mental sphere and the negative events in your existence and the Negative Emotions that "appear" to be caused by the negative events. Briefly, it is a matter of addressing the negative in your momentary experiencing and "owning" it. The awakening human recognizes their responsibility in the creation of negative realities.

Wisdom Lessons, then, refer to this two-step activity. First the researcher, through experimentation and analysis in the laboratory that is the Personal Reality, arrives at Findings specific to their Life Lessons. These Findings may have been "hidden from view" for many years. They represent the hard truth of the developing personality over time. None of you are perfect. The human in physical incarnation may strive for perfection, but that state of being is reserved for other dimensional-experiences.

So the truth is made known through experimentation. What you have been denying is revealed to you in all of its harsh and intense glory. Now what does the awakening human do with this information? In our system the method is clear: with the developing skills of creating Loving Understanding and Courage out of anger, denial and fear, the researcher transforms the difficult material into its divine opposite.

Now this Loving Understanding entails acceptance of the negative Findings on all levels of creaturehood. You are responsible, as I have said earlier. You are the creator of your world and the events within your world. Accepting your responsibility for your creations is the necessary first step here. The second step entails understanding and the gaining of wisdom or Divine Insight. This is accomplished by allowing the Soul Self to perceive your world. The ego/intellect is gently placed to the side and the Higher Consciousness is brought through the portal of creation - the ajna center directly between the eyes. This may be accomplished by meditating or visualizing the Divine as coming though your physical body construct. You will naturally create you own imagery, thought and emotion for this exercise. Throughout the new material I have given you many techniques to accomplish this.

Example - Lessons of Diabetes

Let us provide another example here. To recap for the reader, it is my suggestion that the great majority of human beings realize what are the Lessons they have come to Earth to learn. They are perceived as faint memories by most of you. These distant perceptions are glimpses of the Soul Self as it attempts to penetrate the barrier of the ego/ intellect. These "memories" may indeed be "powered" by the Negative Emotions. That is precisely why you avoid thinking about these Lessons. It is a wholly natural response to the Negative Emotions: avoidance.

Now the example concerns a human in the throes of bringing up to the surface of consciousness their Wisdom Lessons. Perhaps they have avoided thinking about these issues for many years, perhaps the majority of the life lived. However, now it is time to confront this difficult material, come what may. Specifically, let us say that this human has avoided social contact with others to any degree out of fear of being criticized. Perhaps they were criticized relentlessly by others when they were young. This fearful approach has become a lifestyle, forcing the subject to live behind closed doors, in a sense, even though they secretly yearn for human contact.

As we have stated in The Healing Regimen, the diabetic, for example, may be learning Lessons of appreciation and Love with this illness. They have not enjoyed the sweetness that life offers, such as perhaps the social contact so necessary to normal development for the human. To remedy this, it is suggested that one would intentionally LEARN how to appreciate the life being lived. The human would do well to attempt to EMBODY appreciation, to BECOME appreciation. The next simple step would be to courageously transmit this LEARNED emotional state to others intentionally. The sweetness of life is sweet indeed, but only when you notice it and experience it and then "pass it along" to others, to use the vernacular. I am certain that this message from The Seth Entity is appropriate for many of you, beyond those who are "diabetic." To embody the opposite of the Negative Emotions you are experiencing, is a very potent method of magical creation.

Wisdom Lessons and Choice

You always have a choice, Dear Reader. The great question for you as a physical being is this: when you awaken to your true reality, will you choose to create your life of Lessons consciously, or will you try to escape, play hooky from this dramatic enterprise of physical existence? Many of you well know what I am saying in these paragraphs, for you are well on your way to awakening fully. Yet some of you may look on these new essays of mine with the all too critical eye of the ego. Fear, cynicism, competition rule the roost of the ego. I would ask you to pull back from this type of scrutiny and attempt to use the perspective of the "awakened one." The heart is open as anger is transmuted into Loving Understanding. Fear is turned to Courage and faith.

The awakened or enlightened human may choose to be creative with the creation of events within their own reality. You may postpone the event of your physical death, for example, and undergo The Transition at a later date, perhaps learning more and gaining the Divine Knowledge from these additional months or years of living experience.

This is your Life

This is your life, you see. This dramatic and sometimes comedic performance in Earthly flesh is your life, for which you have PURPOSEFULLY incarnated. You are experiencing both the positive and the negative life has to offer. Yes it is true that you inevitably age and die, perhaps being subject to much pain and suffering; yet there is also joy in these sequential moments of your life. With the proper attitude you may even experience your suffering moments in what can be described as "joyful appreciation." This may be difficult to comprehend for some of you. Let us have an example of how this paradox of feeling and behavior might be experienced by any one of you as you go about your meaningful lives.

As you awaken to the Unity of Consciousness Dimension, you will gradually become more aware of your Simultaneous Lives. Within these lives you are living the broad spectrum of existence. Thus, as you retain memories of a life lived within a society as a tortured being who is daily subjected to painful living experiences, you may compare this life with your current existence in the modern world. Do you see how you might experience a sense of joyful appreciation for your current life? Relative to other lives you are living in the midst of great pain and suffering, your current existence may be regarded as joyful and complete.

Punishment?

Now there <u>are</u> times for you, as a researcher and a learner of Lessons, when you may seem to be engaged in ardently co-creating your reality in a very responsible fashion. You are "doing everything right," let us say, and diligently attending to the transformation of Negative Emotions into their divine opposites. You are doing so very well in this endeavor that you perhaps feels as though you should be rewarded in some way, feeling that the Powers That Be could "have mercy" on you, so that you might relax and enjoy yourself for a period of time. Yet let us say that you still continue to experience a challenging existence with a series of quite negative events serving to "drive home" this harsh reality.

"Am I being singled out for punishment," you might ask yourself. Now we must at times such as these, revert back to first principles. You create your own reality. If you are feeling victimized, you are ultimately the tormentor. If you are in the midst of painful, negative personal dramas, you are ultimately the director, the producer and also the cast of these dramas. You are composed of many personality aspects within your Personal Reality ego/intellect. But your greater personality or Higher Consciousness also participates through a lending of energy to the "dramatic flow" of the events in your life. In this way, you are the whole - the cosmos - and you are also the individual living component of the whole. I believe I must elaborate further on this phenomenon for your ULTIMATE understanding. (humorously)

The reason that you sense a familiarity in the scenes of your everyday life, as if all of the characters in these daily dramas of yours are your "relations," is that everyone you meet and interact with moment-to-moment is indeed your relation. The relevant aspects of your Higher Self are reflected through these other personalities relative to the learning of your individual, Soul Family and Entity Lessons. Naturally there would be a familiarity in this dance of synchronicity you know as physical reality. You act in concert, then, at any one time and all of the time, with your cohorts, keeping your appointments with "perfect strangers," to enact your behaviors in the quest for Value Fulfillment. We shall have more to say on this phenomenon in our forthcoming manuscript on the Soul Family.

Divine Knowledge

We often use the phrase in these new messages, "I am not telling you something you do not already know." This is a statement of fact. We are merely reminding you the reader of that knowledge you have acquired in your many voyages into physical form. This information on the nature of reality and the use of energy, you first brought with you from your existence in nonphysical reality, before your "physical" birth into the human body. Now this knowledge also is a part of your FUTURE heritage, if you may understand this conundrum of mine.

Perhaps a better way to describe the relearning phenomenon in which you are engaged is this... bleedthroughs

- the perceptual breakthroughs of your current self into other Simultaneous Lives - occur throughout your waking and dreaming periods. These are learning "field trips" in which your current conscious perception tunes-in on one or more of your past, other current or future lives. This is a function of the multitasking Soul Self as you awaken to your multidimensional experiencing. This is the acquiring of the Divine Knowledge we constantly refer to in these manuscripts.

On a basic level, you already know this material. That is why it seems so familiar to you. That is why it seems so true. You have perfected this system in your numerous future incarnations, again in your familiar terms, assuming the linear time illusion that is favored in your dimension. And so you see, I use the phrase "this you already know" as a device to hopefully trigger memories here. The little bleedthroughs that you experience I hope will keep you motivated enough to continue the voyage with us. These are tools the nonphysical beings use as we attempt to educate humanity. The phrase is a deep and empowered one, a profound suggestion. However, just accept it playfully and see where it leads you. This phrase may help you to wake-up to your greater reality.

Why Pursue the Spiritual?

Let us discuss an issue that is quite obvious. Perhaps that is why we have neglected it thus far in these new writings. The issue may be framed with a question: "Why Seth do you assume that the readers of your new books are looking for spiritual understanding? If the path to Loving Understanding and Soul Evolution is so perilous and fraught with physical and psychological pain, why would anyone in their right mind want to pursue it?" (humorously)

To begin, the readers of my books, as I have observed them over the many years since I first began communications with my First Subject, are seekers. They are drawn to this work, I assume, because it "speaks to them." Others of a different personality style and temperament, perhaps, would be drawn to other Teachings. Now it is true that the older material created with Jane Roberts was quite barren of discussions of spiritual matters. This was an editorial decision. I have continuously offered my spiritually-informed content to humanity. However, since it is the human co-creator of the book who creates the book in physical reality, it is the human co-creator who determines what they consider to be appropriate content for the book.

These new manuscripts are the spiritual - you might say the divine - counterparts to the old material. If you are a student of Seth, to complete your studies you would do well to attend to the spiritually-based material contained in these new books. Now I have attempted to include weighty intellectual discussions in my new work, to satisfy those of you who are focussed on the physical dimension in which you live. The spiritual is merely the other side of this physical dimension. To become a well-rounded, educated human, you would do well to study both aspects of reality.

208

The path to Soul Realization may be thought of as arduous by some. This is true. Certainly it is not for the meek and mild. It is easy to lose confidence and perhaps quit the journey before it has truly begun. As you examine your expanded reality, you most definitely will be experiencing some of your lifetimes within less than ideal circumstances. If you tune-in, for example, to a lifetime in which you are dying slowly from starvation or an illness of some kind, this witnessing may be so distasteful and shocking that you are thrown out of your meditative state. I would suggest that you remember in these cases, under these circumstances of harsh conditions, that you are supported on a wave of ecstasy that is the Soul Self. This ecstasy may help to motivate you to continue your studies.

Now suppose that you are experiencing negative realities within your current life. Should you attempt these explorations of your other Simultaneous Lives? Generally, I would suggest that you first gain some mastery over the exercises and conduct the various experiments I have outlined in my last two books.

After Enlightenment

We have spoken before of the gratifying changes in consciousness that come with Soul Evolution. What we are really talking about here is a systematic approach to belief change. The example we used pertained to a change in belief regarding radial prejudice. In our example, the person had undergone a subtle transformation in consciousness by "working on themselves" to the degree that they no longer feared or hated a particular race or group of people, but they were indeed experiencing growing affection for these people, for the race as a whole. I described this feeling as a form of ambivalence, in that the person still harbored negative feelings for the group of people, but the positive feelings for the group were beginning to overtake the negative. This person was on the cusp of positive belief change. They were comfortable with the uncertainty they were experiencing, for as I said, they were working on themselves, trying to learn their Lessons, and they were, at least for the moment, able to resist recognizing the negative inner dialogue concerning the group of people. They were able to "turn down the volume," you see, on the negative inner dialogue, and "turn up the volume" on their self-created positive inner dialogue. So this is what belief change entails.

The God Book

For our next project together, Mark and I will create The God book - the manuscript on All That Is. We hope to present for you an interesting and educational book on the creative source for all of your realities. However, I believe we would do well to provide you with some of the ideas and theories we will cover in that book, now in this current manuscript, so that you may better absorb and utilize these current messages from The Seth Entity.

Now my First Subject created a book on her conceptualization of the personal God. *(The God of Jane. mf)* This was a very therapeutic exercise for her, in that many of her "demons" from the past were faced, and in a sense, taken "into the light" and disempowered in that way. In these new books of mine, we are presenting the reader with the exercises and experimentation required to pursue a similar course of study.

Obviously, because we are incessantly on the topic of Reality Creation here, the question of "who is the reality creator?" must arise just as incessantly. I do believe that it is more than a mere matter of semantics. Who is the creator of your Personal Reality? I have advised you over these many years that it is indeed YOU the reader of this book who creates your Personal Reality. Now where does God and where do the concepts of the Divine fit within this cosmology of a reality-creating human? Let us discuss this for just a moment...

To begin, you Dear Reader, are the epitome of All That Is. You are composed of divine energy constructs - the CUs. In each and every one of the Consciousness Units you may find the holographic replica of EVERYTHING in all of your created realities. This EVERYTHING we are also referring to as All That Is. Now this metaphor of a holographic reality may serve us well here in this discussion. The simplified definition of a hologram for our purposes might be, "that which is everywhere all of the time." This describes the fundamental nature of the CUs as well as the multidimensional atoms theorized by some of your scientists. The researcher may make practical use of this theoretical construct by experimenting with experiencing the everywhere-all-the-time perspective. This perceptual vantage point is actually each and every Moment Point in space and time, so it does include past, present and future, in your terms.

This All That Is we have named to move beyond religious connotations of any kind. It is a safe generic title, is it not? Yet at the same time, being ALL that is, this construct would naturally hold within itself what we might call the Divine or the sacred or spiritual worlds. The visionary experience treats the researcher, or perhaps the accidental mystic, to the sensory extravaganza that is multidimensional existence. How does one then define this experience in retrospect? Invariably the human bows to authority in these matters, and again as we have discussed in these pages, hands over their powers of Reality Creation to another higher, perhaps "more worthy" entity. Thus the gods and goddesses are born.

We do not intend to trivialize this god-making faculty of the human being. These self-created constructs are definitely "given a life of their own" through the ongoing support of "thought energy" through the prayers and other spiritual observances of countless Souls over the millennia. The personality aspects of the human are constellated "out" onto the physical world from "within." Each of the separate Earthly cultures, then, creates their individual divinities ac-cording to the needs of their particular group. So that the Nordic peoples, for example, developed an entirely different pantheon than did the Indonesian islanders. Different divine beings evolve from the different cultural needs of the people who live in the collective. Now let us relate this to the individual researcher living in your current timeframe.

God is Dead?

It has been broadly suggested by some of you, in a very sensationalist manner, that God is dead. This phrase is quite actually a powerful suggestion. In a way, it represents the triumph of materialism and of science over the human consciousness. However, in truth quite literally, if you are alive, God is not dead. You are the creator of your world. With All That Is you individually create your Personal Reality Field and collectively do you co-create your Consensus World Reality. So perhaps God with a capital G might also be described as the ensemble of humans, animals and elements on Earth at any one time. However, since the whole is to be found within the part in this holographic model of reality, even if you were the last person alive on Earth, God would STILL not be dead.

Our philosophical discussion begs the question, "If I am the creator of my world and All That Is is within each CU or atom in physical reality, does this mean that I am also God or All That Is?" Here again, the issue is not merely one of semantics. Let me explain. Religious conditioning serves to disempower the religion practitioner. We are speaking in broad generalities here. Particularly in your monotheistic practices, it is of course the churchgoer and student of the religious texts who remains in the subservient role. The God with a capital G is the almighty one. No one or thing comes before this God.

Now humility is achieved through the observance of this sacred relationship. Thus you have the humility expressed by the saints and by the disciples in your Christian religion. Yet may I suggest that the great majority of the practitioners of the Christian faith take it much too far, so far indeed that the average Christian in actuality SEPARATES themselves from the Godhead. Through praise of the almighty God, the one and true King of Heaven, the power and spirituality of the practitioner is often overcome and finally forgotten.

The original words of The Christ, if I may be so bold, asked the observer of these fundamental Teachings to participate AS AN EQUAL. As the new religion found followers, and the inevitable rise to power within the church structure of priests and other leaders occurred, this egalitarian relationship with the God was not discussed. Eventually, as the priests consolidated their power, this brotherly and sisterly relationship between the Creator and the created was deemed blasphemous. Those who spoke in terms of their equality with God were punished. We are attempting to change this relationship with these writings. We are reminding the spiritually-minded person of their original relationship with the Godhead.

CHAPTER NINE

The Consensus Reality Field

Dialogue - Truth
6/2/06 2:35 PM

Mark: What is going on in our nation these days?
Seth: Now briefly, your world is in the middle of the Fourth-Dimensional Shift. In your U.S.A. and other countries you risk succumbing to the forces of hatred and totalitarianism. As your election will again demonstrate, the system is broken. The will of the people is subverted. It will take action on the part of many millions of you in the West to turn the tide. You do not have the numbers yet because you are complacent and afraid. But as the media gradually begin to present truthful stories for all to read, your numbers will grow. Act now to help make it happen, Mark. Participate in your community to encourage the truthful representation of reality within your media and within your communities. That is all for now.
Mark: Thanks for the pep talk Seth.

The Consensus Reality Field

The Consensus Reality Field is our term for the broader field of Reality Creation of which you are a part by virtue of your individually created world. Your Personal Reality Field serves you well within your niche in your environment. It is "tailor made" according to your specifics, both conscious and unconscious. Now the broader field of Reality Creation may be thought of as comprising, for example, your neighborhood, your city, your state, your country, your hemisphere and finally your world - the planet Earth.

I will not bore you with more descriptions of how you create the Personal Reality Field. Suffice it to say that you and the others who live in your neighborhood, achieve a consensus while sleeping on what will be created, in so far as your neighborhood goes, upon awakening. Obviously this holds true for the manifestation of your city's Consensus Reality, your state's, and so on.

Negative Media

Now we may discuss affecting the Consensus World Reality from the privacy of your own Personal Reality Field. Just as our advice to "keep a good thought" - a simplistic solution to transform negative realities - was offered to you the reader, this technique of contributing to the Positive Manifestation within the Consensus World Reality from your Personal Reality is offered with just as much surety that you will find success. The simplistic becomes the profoundly effective, as in other examples we have discussed.

Now what are we saying, in so much as we are describing the Positive Manifestation? First let me state emphatically that we are NOT describing the reality presented to you in the media. You well know by now that I am quite impatient with the purveyors of madness and violence and negativity that we refer to as the Negative Media. These media would be the sensationalist newspapers, the warmongering television programs presented as "news," the violent controlling internet websites. These media present what we might call "the accepted" worldview of your deluded leaders and their business associates, the pillagers of your worldly goods, including your natural resources, the stores of your Mother Earth.

This is why you find yourselves prisoners of a quite toxic Consensus Reality, you see. Many of you are using the "templates" offered to you by these Negative Media, to create a negative fearful reality. In a sense, many of you believe it is your "civic duty" to do so.

For example: some of you believe with all of your might that you are a good citizen if you prepare for the "imminent" terrorist attack from your "enemies." And so you stock up on the necessities of life in preparation for a few months or years underground, in your safe room. This is ridiculous my friend. Now I am certainly not speaking to you personally here, I am referring simply to those of you who have fallen under the spell of negative conditioning perpetrated by your leaders and the business interests that "rule" your world.

But let us examine what sort of Consensus Reality you help to create from the "safety" of your safe room. Are you contributing to a world based on Love and the acceptance of your fellow human beings without judgement or fear? I think not. In all probability, you are from your safe room, merely adding to the hatred, adding to the fear, helping to do your part in the perpetuation of negative realities.

Ignoring the Truth

The creation of <u>positive</u> realities is your responsibility. It is a personal issue. Because you are the creator in physical reality, it is a matter of how aware you become of your responsibilities. Now the great majority of you, it is true, will remain in a sleep state, in a manner of speaking, right up until the time of the Dimensional Shift. On the surface it will appear as though you are unaware of the changes that your civilization is going though. Yet for most of you, there will be great changes already underway on the subtle levels. You are being prepared for the transformation in the dreamstate. You are not aware of this, however, as you go about your waking reality. You prefer to "pretend" that life as usual continues to unfold, without any great upheavals to anticipate.

For this group of people the shift will take place overnight, quite literally. They will awaken one day and suddenly appreciate the vast changes they have undergone, as individuals and as parts of the collective. These are of the type of human that wishes to "not think about" the future that much, for the future will "take care of itself." This group comprises many millions of you on your Earth.

To pretend that business as usual is being experienced at this time in your history is a form of denial, a denial of the Soul Self. On the level of the Soul's experiencing, you know full well that great changes are underway for you. Constantly you are reminded of this by Beings of Light as they transmit their messages into your mental sphere. It is a simple matter to ascribe these messages, as we stated in the first chapter of this manuscript, to bad memories or other forms of "negative thinking." Then you may go on your way, blissfully unaware on an ego/intellect level, of what your Soul most surely knows. Let us present an example to make this clear for the reader.

Suppose you are a typical human of the type I am describing. That is, you are one who discounts, perhaps as spiritual hogwash, the statements of your associates that describe the hearing of the voices of dead ancestors. Or else you deny accounts of those who describe the means to avoid a calamity they faced on the highway, as in an accident or some such thing, as coming from a nonphysical source. The intuitive voice is discounted here, you see. These humans may even ascribe the great luck of winners of various prizes or monies from the inside information given to them by their Angels or etheric advisers to mere coincidence. They deny the voice of the sacred in the lives of others, and so they must be consistent as they deny the voice of the sacred within their own lives.

219

The Ugly American

Millions of you are assisted in your denial of the sacred by your leaders, by your nation, by your colleagues. This is why you continue to suffer the negative outcomes of your Consensus Reality creations. Excuse me for just one moment while I speak directly to those of you in the U.S.A. on the subject of "the ugly American."

It may well make you feel uneasy as I describe to you the shadow of your once great country. It is the negative counterpart to the positive expressions of your America. You will not hear of these discussions in your mass media, the Negative Media I have just described for you. This is the unofficial version of what has come from your actions as a nation upon the world stage.

With your very negative actions at this time, you are quite effectively preventing the manifestation of the New World - the Unity of Consciousness Dimension - within your collective awareness. Your country, through your several wars, through your Negative Media and propaganda, through the tainting of your very culture with the evil of your leaders who have no sense for what is right for the people or the country, is preventing the perceptual breakthrough into the Fourth Dimension that I have been discussing with you in these new messages.

There are many of you who believe the lies told to you by your misguided leaders. It is true, often it is much easier to believe a lie. That is why many of you believe that all is well with your leaders and your country. For to question that authority would force you to acknowledge that the reality for you is just the opposite of the propaganda. Who wants to admit that they have been swindled? Who would easily admit that they were wrong on matters of such great importance? It is a very, very important task to find and admit the TRUTH in these matters. For when the truth is found and acknowledged, only then does the work begin. All of the years of lies and manipulation have left you with a stagnant culture. The Soul's evolution has been cut short. It is now time to begin your individual and collective transformation.

Projections

Now this process begins with you. You are connected to everything in the created Universe through a divine relationship between the CUs that make up your physical and etheric body and the CUs that combine to create those Reality Constructs that "seem" to reside outside of your consciousness. You only appear to be separate. You only seem to be disconnected from your environment. In actuality, your entire exterior world is first within you - within your creative consciousness or mind. We have spoken of this essential within-ness of your world. Each and every physical Reality Construct is "born" from an idea within you that is cast upon your outside world, much as a motion picture projector casts the images onto a screen for your perception. This you already know.

Now these projections of physical reality serve a purpose for you individually, for others in your Soul Family and for those in your greater Soul Family - humanity. Much as you might learn a lesson from an educational film at your school, you learn your life Lessons from the self-created "projections" of your ultimately creative human consciousness.

You might be thinking to yourself, "Wonderful! I am connected to everything. This is a good theory to think about, but how can I use it practically in my daily life?" Of course, you are already using this knowledge in your everyday life. You are just doing so unconsciously in a rote fashion. Knowing and accepting that you are the creator of your world may allow you to experiment with conscious creation. You will in fact be consciously co-creating your Soul's agenda for learning. Victimhood falls away when such a perspective is established within your human mentality. Also, of course, you gain the great responsibility for creating positive Loving realities for the greater good of all.

The Individual is Important

I refer the reader to our book on Soul Evolution for a discussion on the value of the individual human consciousness in the collective conversation that we are calling the Telepathic Network. One person can truly make a difference here in this Consensus Reality. It could well be your single Loving thought - expressed in the telepathic conversation - that could tip the scales to the positive manifestation. Imagine how powerful your Loving thoughts could be when joined by hundreds, thousands, millions of other Loving thoughts directed intentionally by LOVERS of your Mother Earth. There is certainly power in numbers in these matters. And that is what it shall take... huge numbers of Lovers of the Earth using their powerful thoughts of creation on the subtle levels to creative positive realities.

So the individual is important. The individual expression of Loving energy directed toward the creation of a positive reality - world peace for example - is what will save you from yourselves. All of your thoughts of Love are acknowledged, you see. Each Loving thought matters. They have a cumulative effect also, so that a momentum is built over time, such that the creation of the positive reality might well become inevitable.

Incidently, in recent years you have used your Loving thoughts in concerted ways to make profound changes in your waking realities. Great disasters were averted. Calamities that would have claimed many hundreds of thousands of lives were "de-energized" and so were not manifested.

It is true that your world has seen recent Earth Changes that entailed great loss of life. What I am suggesting is that there was the potential for many more disasters to occur entailing many more casualties. As a consensus of reality creators, then, you and your fellow occupants of the planet agreed to manifest and then did manifest an altered reality. You saved yourselves, you see. This phenomenon happens quite often, though you do not realize it for you are not yet awakened fully. You do not yet acknowledge your full creative powers. However, you soon shall.

Prelude to Navigating the Consensus Reality Field

The following experiment has as its objective, accessing the state of emerging reality we are calling the Consensus Reality Field. This is indeed a timeless experiencing, for you are within the webwork of creation in a pre-manifestation stage of awareness. Time as you think of it - linear time - does not exist. In this state of awareness you will be cultivating, you will witness the emerging reality of the moment. As you know, the moment is all you have, Dear Reader. The moment is all there truly is. It is only the emotional attachments to past, present and future moments that keep you tied to the wheel of life - the continuous unfolding of "events." So this awareness we are asking you to develop exists beyond time as you understand it. This state may be experienced through the use of the Inner Senses or Intuition.

This Reality Field is vast within your current Moment Point. For this reason, the researcher must narrow the focus of study to a simple line of inquiry. The world reality expressed in the "historical narrative," you might say, includes the reputed "true" narratives of the various mass media of your planet. From this soup of converging "facts," incidents, ideas and images, emerges what we are describing in this book as the status quo or Consensus World Reality.

So this Gestalt of Consciousness is largely a product of your Negative Media. Are you beginning to understand my point here? If you as a Scientist of Consciousness are to adequately access, understand and change for the better your perceived Consensus World Reality, you must certainly be at first very skilled in focusing on your subject. If you are not ultimately focused and strong in this endeavor, you will be "blown away" - a metaphor we have used before - by the energy, ideas and images you will face in this experiment.

You must be strong. The negative energies that seek to dominate your world are quite formidable, in that they are energized through the tapping into of fear within the population. Fear, hatred, anxiety, ruthlessness... these are the states of consciousness that feed the growth of the Negative Entities. So you must be fairly adept at transforming fear and anxiety into Courage, Loving Understanding and personal power. You must have reached an advanced state of self-awareness so that you will not be overcome when you enter the arena in which these Entities exist.

Now as we have also documented in these writings, the Beings of Light, in a sense "riding" on a wave of benevolent energy - Love and Courage - are also active in the domain of Consensus World Reality creation. These Higher-Dimensional Beings and Spiritual Masters - Gestalts of Consciousness energized by the Loving energies of generations upon generations of "do-gooders" from your planet Earth and elsewhere - are actively confronting the Negative Beings on these levels of consciousness.

I trust you are with me so far. This may now all seem like a colorful fairytale for some of you. Please know that I am presenting this information to you in a fashion so that more are inclined to understand than deny.

Experiment - Navigating the Consensus Reality Field
Hypothesis: you may contribute to the positive manifestation of world realities.

Perform your Ritual of Sanctuary

Relax. Achieve your Trance State. You are a member of the Seth Entity. You are in active alliance with the Entity through reading this material. Knowing this, follow your Intention - your Divine Will - down into your personal Underworld with the full expectation of witnessing the creation of Global Consensus Realities. If you encounter Negative Beings of any type, strengthen your Sanctuary of protection with your Intention. Pass through these domains of confusion and control. When you experience a sense of peace, Loving Understanding and a strong sense of the other Virtues of humanity, attempt to perceive with your Inner Senses the activities within this domain. You may well have reached the Consensus Reality Field of the Positive Manifestation we speak about in these books. If you receive confirmation that you have arrived, let your own positive ideas, images, beliefs and emotions serve to strengthen and validate this phenomenon. See the New World of peace and Loving Understanding begin to solidify and materialize within Third-Dimensional Reality. Return to surface awareness.

Findings - Document your discoveries.

CHAPTER TEN

The Vanguard Leads

Dialogue - Multitasking
6/2/05 9:17 AM

Mark: I am surrounded by people in a public setting. Can you come through with some information to see if I can take your dictation in public?

Seth: Mark, I am just below the surface for you today. I am transmitting clues into your consciousness and so into your physical environment. The woman in front of you was talking about a man named "Seth." You heard it right. You have your feet in both worlds here. You exemplify, through these "translation" activities, particularly in public, as you are doing now, the contact with Beings of Light that we are encouraging in our books.

Group Effort

You are the Vanguard. As I have discussed previously, you have in all probability incarnated this time around to fulfill your obligations once again as an advocate for your Mother Earth and for humanity.

Believe me when I say this... it will take many hundreds of thousands of you to turn the tide of negativity and destruction on your world. Yet that is exactly what I propose in these writings... that those of you who read my words here and understand them, call upon your friends and family and business associates who may be of a similar mind as you, to join us in this Research Project - the creation of positive realities.

As I have suggested to Mark, popularity of my new works will grow as readers tell their friends and associates that I have returned. Word of mouth is a powerful catalyst. Yet the majority of newly enlightened members of this family of ours will already be engaged on the subtle levels. Telepathy is the communication network on the Etheric Planes and all of you are well-versed in this system.

Additionally, of course, you also create worlds both probable and actual with your powerful thoughts. And so you see, this is the method. This is how we shall recreate the current Consensus Reality into one more attuned to the positive aspects of humanity: Love, compassion, Courage.

Soul Family Through Time

Now these groupings of humans engaged in concerted collective efforts, such as this Vanguard, exist over time. For purposes specific to the group, members will incarnate during the same timeframe, and experience the Value Fulfillment achieved through their activities. For example: a group of religious devotees who incarnate in the time of the prophets to study and worship as a collective, may upon death of the physical form, go on a sabbatical of sorts in the Home Dimension and others, and not obtain a physical body for hundreds of years. This group may then take on bodies as a group of scientists working on a problem in physics within one of your universities in your present timeframe.

Soul Family groupings exist at all "levels" of consciousness manifestation. Consciousness creates realities. What you might call "negative" or "cynical" or perhaps "regressive" consciousness, therefore, seeks out opportunities to create negative, cynical, regressive realities, again, for purposes of fulfilling these particular values. So at any one point in your history, you see, you may have unfolding many different mass movements of Reality Creation upon your planet.

Currently, for example, you have the movement of healers, lightworkers, your New Agers who share the planet and your timeframe with the practitioners of the extreme opposites of these values. I trust I am not appearing unnecessarily vague. You know what I mean here, Dear Reader. You have your work cut out for you, to coin a phrase. Your gains in fulfilling values of Loving Understanding, Courage, compassion and the like, will of necessity come at a "price," in your view of things. There is no good or evil, only your thinking makes it so, to again coin a phrase for illustration. Yet thinking and consideration and study are precisely what are required here. This means finding distinctions, marking off where you stand ethically, as perhaps "opposed" to other ethical standards. Certainly you will be waging <u>what appears</u> to be a war against evil, of good against evil. Yet may I remind you here, since all is one, you are in essence merely confronting your own "unacceptable" self. You are always reacting to your own projections. Here you are reacting to the projecting of your personality aspects out onto the world.

Keeping a Good Thought

Now those among you who find yourselves called to act within your social groups, will find your paths are cleared of obstacles to progress. Soul progression is the order of the day, you see. This divine attitude is therefore reflected within your Personal and Collective Reality Fields. It is really as simple as "keeping a good thought," as the saying goes. Is this simplistic New Age wishful thinking? Yes it is (humorously), simple and direct and extremely powerful.

This series we titled *Communications from Seth on the Awakening of Humanity* for a very good reason. The simple act of keeping a good thought, when observed ritually by many thousands of humans, will lead to the creation of positive Loving realities that are the catalyst for the mass-awakening of humanity. So again, the simple, the basic becomes the profoundly effective exponentially, as you, for example, remind your co-workers to focus on the positives, the Loving outcomes of the daily work activities. Or when you teach your young child the simple skill of focusing on the positives, as a basis for the creation of positive outcomes. The simple becomes the profound, my friend.

Back to Love

In this transformation your Mother Earth is healing herself by "throwing off" the harmful parasites that have plagued her. The negative leaders, the corrupt business officials, the violent among you are now being "processed" by the TRUE powers that be. These powers are the Higher Consciousness - the higher selves of these humans. Let me go further with this, as my associate Mark is suggesting to me that I elaborate upon a brief Holographic Insert I imparted to him moments ago. This inspirational illustration I transmitted into Mark's mental environment, concerned an example of spiritual transformation that is well underway with many thousands of your fellow citizens who are members of mainstream religions.

Let me first say that ALL expressions of the Divine within human consciousness, are what you might call "legitimate" or "worthy" expressions. All That Is seeks to know itself through the spiritual expressions of human beings within their simple religious practices, that you might experience when you ask for help from the Divine in a simple personal matter, as in prayer that your operation will be successful, and through their more complex and obvious spiritual practices, such as you might see within the walls of your great churches, as hundreds join in the contemplation of the Divine in prayer and other rituals. So it is all divine, you see. Everything is born out of the divine and Loving energies of All That Is. Now the key word here is Loving. Where there is devoted unconditional Loving powering these practices of the Divine, there will be Soul Evolution in these groups of practitioners. For as you well know as a reader of my works, what we are calling Love with a capital L is the veritable creative force of the Universes.

Wherever the path of devotion in any religious practice or "spiritual" practice if you prefer, takes a divergent path from the foundational energies of Love, there will be corrective measures instituted within the consciousness of the sole practitioner or within the group consciousness of the church members. These corrective energies serve to direct the spiritual expression back to one of Love with a capital L.

In our new books I have been critical of your priests and other leaders within your religious hierarchies for playing upon the fears and prejudices of the church members, particularly within your mainstream religions. Some of these leaders have knowingly led the people astray by bringing politics into the church. The cause of Love has been forgotten within these groups as the leaders seek to curry favor with powerful politicians and other secular leaders. These religious leaders, as we add to this manuscript, are engaged in a Turnabout also, just as the many of you who have been engaged in the negative practices - fear mongering, hatred -

are engaged in a Turnabout. With the assistance of the Energy Personalities associated with individuals within these groups and within these hierarchies of control and power, these personalities are being directed back to Love with a capital L. Currently you are just able to see a few of these Turnabouts in your media, as some journalists seek to report the truth of the matters at hand. By the time we publish this third book of ours, this Turnabout will be well underway for many of you, with truly global - and need I say, multidimensional - implications.

My advice to you, if you feel that you are engaged in this Turnabout, is that you allow yourself to go back to Love. If you witness your Earthly associates obviously engaged in this transformation, assist them in finding their way back to Love. You do this by demonstrating within your own Personal Reality Field, the practice of Loving Understanding.

Speaking Your Truth

There is another cliche that is useful for us here in our work - "speaking your truth." This idea of speaking your truth is a very powerful Idea Construct. Indeed, it is revolutionary in its activity within your system. Here again is an example of a simple idea becoming quite profoundly effective when utilized by large groups of humans. The personal also becomes the political here, if you see my meaning. It is the ultimate political act of liberation to speak your truth, Dear Reader. This act is the precise opposite of ceding your powers of Reality Creation to those in authority.

To remind you of my previously expounded upon thoughts on this matter (humorously)... traditionally, the typical human cedes their powerful energies of Reality Creation to those in authority - parent, teacher, employer, politician, priest, scientist, movie star - in exchange for subtle gifts. These gifts are acceptance to the group, permission to keep employed, and so on. Now everything works quite nicely thereafter. The system - essentially a system of control - goes merrily along its way, the citizen believing that they are the "captain of their ship" of individual human consciousness. Obviously this is merely a dream that one hopes to be true.

Now on the other hand, it is true that there are many benefits you receive when you cede your power to those in authority. You receive all of those benefits bestowed upon you by those in power. And it would be unwise to relinquish those benefits of association with the group. Let us see if we may devise a system of speaking your truth in such a way that you are not branded as a nonconformist or a witch. There are quite legitimate ways to speak authentically to those in power without threatening your place within the group. We shall cover this technique next.

Technique - Speaking to the EP of Another

As you change your reality to reflect your awakening Soul, those around you are most probably becoming accustomed to your transformation. This gradual process of transformation from the unaware - the status quo - to the enlightened - the Vanguard - may not be noticed by those in your group for what it is, a revolutionary adaptation of your human consciousness. Those in your group will not be startled, therefore, by the changes in your personality.

As an explorer within these groups of humans, you may use your Inner Senses to determine how you may best interact with any one of your associates. By speaking to the Energy Personality of the human in front of you, you may assess where that person is, within this context of the awakening of the Soul Self. I should say that it is your Higher Self, your Energy Personality, that is doing the assessing here. You are using your Inner Senses that are the perceptive powers of your Soul Self to determine the stage of evolutionary progression of the Soul of any particular human within your group. Now you have always had these powers of perception available to you. Yet only now are you able to use them responsibly.

This technique is simple enough. When you are not sure of the motives of the human in front of you, to get a clearer picture of where they stand - ethically, on the subjects that truly matter to you - you simply assess them via their Energy Personality. If you are not allowed entry, do not press the matter. If you are allowed in, simply ask what are the ethical standards for this human. This skill, as are all the others, is sharpened with use.

We will now present our final experiment of this book.

Experiment - Anticipating the Positive Future
Hypothesis: by anticipating the positive future you create it.

Anticipation occurs in the spacious moment. In past manuscripts I have defined for you the Moment Point and the Point of Power. These are terms that describe the current full moment in your present co-creation activities. Simply, it is your Moment Point if you say it is, Dear Reader. (humorously) You are bringing your Intention and power to bear on the manifestation phenomenon in the present moment.

Perform your Ritual of Sanctuary

Relax and attain your Trance State. You might experiment with achieving this through linking the divine state of consciousness to sitting down in your comfortable chair or wherever you hold your meditations.

Now... you are in your Moment Point. Your Point of Power exists NOW as your portal to affecting your future IN A POSITIVE WAY. Imagine before you all the positive realities you have created while working with this material. The ecstasy just below the surface of consciousness supports you. The contact with the Divine may be experienced as a tingling sensation between your physical eyes. All of your Guides and Helpers, known and unknown, surround you and support you. Bring all of your Inner Senses into this exercise to enliven it and strengthen the manifestation. Stay with it for a few minutes. Return to surface awareness.

Findings - Document your experiences.

Exercise - Consolidate your Findings

While working with the many techniques and experiments provided for you in this book, you have no doubt had differing outcomes of success. You are an individual with individual educational needs. Hopefully you are taking what serves you best and incorporating it into your Reality Creation agendas.

In this final exercise we are asking you to make a list of those techniques and experiments that have helped you the most in the creation of positive realities and in the learning of Lessons. Please take a few minutes to go over your notes and Findings and assemble the material that "speaks to you" most strongly and authentically here. This should be a pleasant and easy exercise. The material that did not work quite well enough for you may be saved for another day. For now, simply make your list of five to possibly ten relevant Findings and particularly successful outcomes of the techniques and experiments we have offered you in these pages.

Document Your Findings Here

_____

_____

_____

_____

_____

_____

_____

_____

_____

_____

Epilogue

Positive Thinking

In conclusion, you shall have success in creating positive realities to the degree that you hold positive thoughts within your mental environment. This habit of positive thinking is your foundation for the creation of an improved Personal Reality. Now as you know, you are ONE with all of humanity through the interconnectedness of the Consciousness Units. And so, as you do your part here, and others of like mind and behavior do theirs, the whole of humanity is influenced in a very positive fashion.

Keep a good thought, Dear Reader. Nourish Loving Understanding and Courage within your consciousness. Challenge the toxic status quo reality with your powerful thoughts of forgiveness and compassion.

Your world is on the verge of a breakthrough into multidimensional perception. You may assist others by leading through example in all that you say and do. Regardless of your own perceived "station" in society, regardless of your perceived "faults," regardless of any history you may have of creating negative realities for yourself and others, you may in this current moment set the stage for future continuous positive reality creations, for your own sake, and certainly for the sake of all beings that share the planet with you. Thank you for participating with us in The Research Project. We will have more to discuss with you in our future manuscripts. Until then, good bye.

QUESTIONS AND ANSWERS WITH SETH

The Third Book
2/11/05 9:38 AM

Seth, could you speak on the Third Book? How will it be produced and when?

Yes Mark. A moment... the Third Book, tentatively titled Thought Reality, is already underway. The material is being formatted within the current timeframe that you occupy, so that we both may "consider" the data into reality. This consideration is the collaboration that you and I use to create material.

Now the Third Book will be a return to the quantum physics material of many years ago. However, we shall be updating those messages with new material that will be illuminated for the understanding of the average reader. As I have said before, this book shall be a step up in intellectual aspects from the Second Book. The Seth readers of old will begin to nose around as we release the Third Book material. Yet the spiritual aspects shall be there, no doubt. The change will be in the acceptance by the intellectuals of the necessarily "Soul-based" presentation of these new messages. All of you are beginning to realize the value of spirit matters. So the early Sethites are changing their ways. They are opening up, Mark.

Alarming Statistics
5/19/05 10:53 AM

You spoke of the role of negative statistics in the creation of disease in The Healing Regimen. Could you say a bit more about this influence?

Let us have an example here. Suppose our theoretical person, one of your contemporaries, an average human on your planet, were to be reading on your Internet or in one of your newspapers and came across an alarming statistic that proclaimed that most people who have a certain "illness" will die within a certain period of time.

Now let us examine what transpires in the thought reality of this person, as they read these alarming statistics. First, if they believe this "scientific" data, they may in all likelihood experience a complete assault upon their consciousness by the negative energies. The forces of depression and disease would be brought to bear upon them. They are opened up, you see, by the negative information, and fear is allowed to plant its seed within this subject's consciousness. This negative information acts as corroboration for this person to create and accentuate "symptoms" within their body. The forces of negativity within this Negative Medium are therefore allowed to control this subject's creation of unhealthy conditions within their body consciousness. Now this is instantaneous. The dis-ease is supported and recreated THE MOMENT that our subject reads the "statistical" figures from the medical "authorities," which may be drug manufacturers, hospitals, doctors and others who may have a vested interest in perpetuating the illness they are describing.

Do you see how your medical establishment, through their manipulative media, conditions you, Dear Reader, into generating and sustaining "illness and disease" within your sacred body? Do you see how you allow this to happen? You are allowing the medical establishment to create realities of symptoms, disease and death.

Soul Family Affiliations
1/23/07 9:48 AM

Do Soul Family affiliations and allegiances change over the course of a lifetime?

Now the answer of course is "Yes." These relationships do change dramatically over time. I have given you some background on this recently in some personal information, *(Seth is referring to a shocking incident*

243

*with someone we thought of as a Soul Family member.
mf)* and now I shall expound upon this topic.

Your Soul Family relationships represent the "proving ground" for the working-out of Soul issues and Lessons. Now keeping it simple here, once the issues are resolved, the Lessons learned to a particular degree of Value Fulfillment, there would be less need, less urgency for the relationship to continue with the Soul Family member, and so that member might well, perhaps gradually over time or quite abruptly, "leave" the Soul Family.

This member who has learned what they have entered the Soul Family to learn, may suddenly become unavailable for physical interactions, for example, by being transferred to another location on your Earth due to business matters. Any such "reasons" for leaving the family would do, and all would appear to proceed in a quite natural manner, for these affiliations are understood by all participants on the subtle levels. However, on the physical level there may be much confusion and intrigue as to why these often intense and mysterious relationships develop and dissolve.

As you know, you need not have a genetic link to Soul Family members. The linkages are metaphysical. Often it is only in retrospect that the importance of the Soul Family relationships are understood. I am sorry that I cannot be more specific. I am leaving it up to the reader - the researcher in physical reality - to look for these connections, to study these relationships and to learn these Lessons.

New Age Concepts
11/24/06 10:12 AM

Seth, why the emphasis on New Age concepts? Are you concerned that the scientific community might object?

Mark your thoughts are well taken. However, these are the basics here. Love and Light are at the base of your Reality Construction. The lightworkers and other healers are quite correct, you see. It is ALL about Light and the use of Light. Now we are giving it a definite Sethian spin, as we must. It is my material after all. But when you examine even my collected works from long ago, you will notice that I covered the same subject matter then as now. I am now simply utilizing the nomenclature of the New Ager. I attempt to speak in the vernacular, in a manner of speaking (humorously), whenever and wherever I present my ideas.

As you know, I have been at this now for many years, in many different contexts, on your Earth and in other systems. I am using this particular strategy because you are familiar with the New Age concepts and vocabulary and many of our new readers are also familiar. I am setting us apart from some of the more "scientifically-minded" of you, I realize. But as you know, I believe we are better off if we avoid this group altogether. This is the New Science we are describing. The proselytizers of the Old Science will soon be forgotten as the millions of you awaken in this timeframe.

Whitehead and Seth
9/15/06 12:16 PM

DP via the Internet asked Seth about the similarity he sees in Seth's material and the theories of philosopher Alfred North Whitehead.

You are correct in your noticing of the similarities in the work of Whitehead and my own. Each generation develops and maintains communications with Beings of Light in similar ways. The expression in written works such as you describe is similar also. Each reflects the spirit of the times in which it was created.

Now these Energy Bodies we are discussing in the new material exist outside of time as you know it, as you PERCEIVE it. Yet each of these multitudinous Energy Forms or Light Bodies develops along their individual evolutionary paths, just as you do, dear reader of this missive. The Energy Body, what we are referring to in the new material as the Energy Personality, evolves as their human counterparts evolve. Indeed, these Light Bodies may be thought of as future expressions of their human counterparts, for they are always "one step ahead" in terms of consciousness development.

As I state in the new material, you as a race are at the end of a thousands-of-years cycle in your development. Just as the Beings of Light increased their communications with humanity during the period you refer to as the Age of the Prophets, so too are they "turning up the volume" in your current timeframe. This is the spirit of the times. Your literature will naturally reflect the stepped-up pace of interdimensional communications.

It would be a mistake, I believe, to study and internalize this phenomenon as a student of comparative religions or philosophy would, as you may miss the message. Certainly the message here is to explore your current existence IN DEPTH, using your Inner Senses. It would not be surprising if you were to do so, that you would come up with Findings that would completely support Whitehead and myself also.

The spirit of the times is a call to individuals, in the West in particular, to seek out and establish communications with your Energy Personalities and begin to explore your personal and the collective consciousness.

(See Chapter Three on Seth's redefining of the term percept, a term Whitehead uses in his papers. I was first drawn to Whitehead's works in the 70's, shortly after I had been introduced to the Seth material. Seth has recently told me that these encounters with Whitehead and the question from DP are all demonstrations of the holographic nonlinear quality of Reality Creation. Seth is inferring that my happening upon the Whitehead book in a college library decades ago "set the stage" for my fielding the question from DP and for Seth's redefining of the term percept for this book. mf)

Negativity?
11/23/06 10:16 AM

Seth, what purpose does negativity serve in the role of enlightenment? This is a question from a Lecture participant.

Briefly... in our new books we are covering this topic of negativity and the search for the Divine. You seem to be expressing the tendency, one that you share with many of your fellow humans, to struggle with negativity.

Now as background, let me remind you that you are all of you created out of Love. All That Is is quite literally, "Love in action." Within a context of Reality Creation we are calling the Love Light Matrix, consciousness seeks to know itself through the creation of ideas into realities. So you are conceived in Love and every atom or Consciousness Unit within your self-created realities is also conceived in Love. Period. Yet the counterpoint to Love must exist to allow Reality Creation to unfold in ways other than Love. Thus you have the Negative Emotions that you are quite familiar with as a human experiencing your life.

The evolution of your human and elemental consciousness proceeds in this way. Your dilemma is the essence of the challenge for humanity. You are all to experience your lives in Third-Dimensional Reality, responding to Love and the opposites of Love. In short, your challenge is to transform the Negative Emotions you may be experiencing into their divine opposites. Thus, you would turn anger and fear into Loving Understanding and Courage. This is fairly simple to state yet profoundly difficult to accomplish consistently. That is why I have returned to publishing, to assist you in this endeavor.

Gracie the Cat and Pets
2/22/07 8:35 AM

Seth, we just recently experienced the death of our beloved little cat Gracie. What can you tell us about the Transition and post-Transition experiences of animals?

I am quite sorry for the loss of your friend. As you know Mark, I share in your experiences to a degree when you allow this, and so I also suffer this loss. Now specifically, your cat Gracie was a "rescue" cat as you well know. Your mate was drawn to that specific animal to keep her "appointment" with your Gracie. This agreement was made on the subtle levels between what you might call the animal Soul of the cat and the Soul Selves of both you and Carol. And so you both experienced an instant recognition on seeing this despondent, fearful kitty in the cage at your pet store and in the foster parent's home.

Now also here, in that instant of recognition, you experienced future probable experiences with yourself, Carol and the cat. These knowing experiences included the probable death of your Gracie within circumstances of time, space and behavior quite similar to those in which Gracie expired. As in all experiences in Third-Dimensional Reality, Value Fulfillment was achieved by all of you in nursing the cat back to an acceptance and Love for humans.

The reciprocal activity here is caring, being cared for, the sharing of Love back and forth, these types of emotional expression and Reality Creation. Again specifically, this cat is currently experiencing an extra-dimensional existence within her animal Soul Family, this time with the added Soul knowledge of what it is to be truly loved, to be truly cared for, as a counter to the traumatic emotional experiencing of being abandoned and abused.

Generally now, your pets are, in a sense, your animal friends "for eternity." Let me explain... you create your reality in cooperation with everything else - All That Is - within your Personal Reality Field. This cooperative venture includes your animal friends, as they are composed of Consciousness Units just as you are, and they also have certain Lessons to learn in physical existence. Previously I have related to you that ALL of your Reincarnational Existences are similar - very much like one another - for YOU are the multidimensional co-creator of these many lives. Naturally there would be similarities.

Thus, for example, suppose one of our readers is examining this volume of ours with a Loving pet - a dog, a cat or other creature - sleeping beside them. If this reader were to briefly engage their Inner Senses for a short exploratory trip to one of their ongoing lives within a different timeframe, a different body and a different confluence of experiences, the reader may witness their beloved pet within an entirely different animal body, perhaps even of a different species, sleeping quietly next to this Reincarnational Self.

I do hope that my cursory description will bring some comfort to you Mark and Carol, and also to those of our readers who are grieving over their Transitioning animal friends. You are all on a similar voyage - the animals, including the human animals of Earth. You are all engaged in the dear appreciation of physical existence in the companionship of one another.

Health Issues
5/6/06 10:57 AM

Mark, let us have some personal material for you, if you agree of course.
Great Seth.

Now then, you and your mate are experiencing physical health issues. These are Lessons for the Soul, of course, and you are in a moment-to-moment agreement with this manifestation on a Soul level. So does it not make sense that you must act on a Soul level to change the manifestation? Now here you may have an ambivalence, you see. The Soul incarnates to learn these Lessons, yet your ego may find the conditions distasteful or perhaps unnecessary. This ambivalence leads to a continuation of the Lesson Mark.

The Subconscious Manifestation Energy Stream has a momentum that supersedes or overpowers the ego. If you wish to change your Lessons "in mid stream," as it were, you must carefully assess the conditions from a Soul perspective. Then you may determine if you wish to learn these Lessons on other levels of consciousness, in other lives etc.; etc.; etc. This takes determination and an open attitude. You must also consider whether it is a good idea or perhaps not a good idea to let the manifestation of health issues continue, for the greater experiencing of All That Is and your Soul Self.

You are in charge here. You may wish to experiment with these ideas, play with the recreation of physical symptoms into healed states or spontaneously healed states of physical awareness. Your mate may also take this advice. More later if you wish.

War
4/14/07 12:00 NOON

Bill V. asks: Can we assume All That Is finds value even with war? Is the Soul concerned with character here? How does this war dynamic work?

Bill you may find value in terms of my concept of Value Fulfillment, if I may make a pun here. Now as I have stated to you readers of my new material, the manifestation process in the Third Dimension is a matter of Value Fulfillment "to the nth degree." Simply, as each Consciousness Unit "expresses" it's innate "personality," in so far as its contribution to the created Reality Construct is concerned - be it computer screen, rug, or even pre-manifested Idea Constructs - it does so according to a sort of "agenda" or "trajectory of development," as we have also expressed it. At the direction of Gestalts of Consciousness of various kinds, the CU's assemble into Reality Constructs that also merge with one another to create your Personal Reality Field. Now everything is conscious, everything is composed of Consciousness Units. So within this context of a Telepathic Network, rapport is achieved among ALL participants in this Reality Creation, according to the contributions of each and every CU as it seeks to experience its individual level or intensity of Value Fulfillment.

Now this blade cuts both ways here. Consciousness seeks to experience itself in physical form. Period. This would include the creation of negative as well as positive realities, in your terms. So that a Soul would come to experience Earthly reality within the body of a baby, knowing on the Soul level that there was a high probability that they would perish in a war. Indeed, Souls SEEK OUT these types of existences and Transitions, to obtain a sort of "breadth of experience" for the greater Soul Self - the Entity, you see.

Everything has its place in the physical world. There are reasons for everything, as your metaphysical philosophers have stated. Most assuredly the researcher would have to of necessity delve deeper in their analysis of the negative realities to find the "causes." However, when they are successful, they will always find that the causes are consciousness. The negative realities are born from the negative thoughts and emotions of human beings.

Christ's Disciple Paul
3/13/07 11:26 AM

From Louise in Spain via the Internet. The most recurring question at the moment is about Paul's presence in this New Era and which signs should I look for?

I will answer Louise's question with reference to material I first transmitted to humanity through my First Subject. A moment... now your biblical Paul was in fact a historical personage, in that this Soul did incarnate on your Earth during biblical times and did indeed engage in the activities for which he is renowned. Remember though, that ALL of the personalities who contributed to your biblical stories, were first and foremost, Souls in physical bodies. They were, like yourself, Dear Reader, experiencing their Lessons in physical reality for the greater learning and Value Fulfillment of their Soul, of their Entity and for All That Is.

Paul was, in particular, as were several others involved in these reincarnational dramas, quite cognizant of his "mission" in that lifetime. He was experiencing his physical reality through the eyes of his Soul Self, in other words. Now the Entity of Paul, a Gestalt of Consciousness that included, for example, all of the personalities known as the

Twelve Apostles and many more also, may be conceived of as a greater Soul Family for purposes of explanation here. You are reading my words in these new books. You know what I mean when I refer to the Soul Family. So remember that the incarnational "itineraries" for Entities and Soul Families are cyclical. These groups of Souls incarnate within the same eras over linear time, to experience physical existence together, to learn their Lessons together. ALL of the "players" within the biblical reincarnational drama are again experiencing physical existence on Earth at this time.

Now let me elaborate on that point here... though they are experiencing physical existence on your Earth, they are also available for contact and communication as Guides. So that the experiments and exercises we have described to you in our new books, may be used to contact these various Guides or Energy Personalities, Beings of Light and so on, at your leisure. Many of you are doing just that.

Louise, this spirit of Paul speaks to you over the centuries. This guide is a relation to you, in a sense, in that you are a part of the greater Paul Soul Family, just as Paul is a member of the Entity that is comprised of these biblical figures. The signs you are looking for are all around you. They may be felt as energy signatures of Paul with the Inner Senses during meditation on the Pauline aspect of The Christ, or however you conceive this Loving articulate Energy Body. As you tune-in to the Pauline transmission stream, you will be, in effect, "overshadowed" by this divine energy. Just as I overshadow Mark in our transmissions, you may be overshadowed and receive the communication stream from the Pauline Energy Body.

Other readers may interpret their experiences with Paul in different ways. You are all different. You will receive what you need to learn your Lessons. Just as I advised the readers of our new books to perhaps adopt our Teaching as an adjunct to their current spiritual practices, I encourage you Louise to keep the essence of your Christianity and observe your observances as you see fit. Take as little or as much as you require from our humble offerings, to "fill out" your practice. This is Christian mysticism in action.

4-D Shift
8/30/07 4:06 PM

Seth, could you give the readers a timeline for the Fourth-Dimensional Shift? Also, is this shift what some are referring to as the singularity and the 2012 phenomenon?

Yes Mark, as I related to you several months ago, your 2007 was to be a watershed year with regards to the Fourth-Dimensional Shift. Now you are well through that time period and perhaps you may see what I meant by that statement. Your world, particularly in the West now, is at this moment in the middle of this shift into the Unity of Consciousness Dimension. You do not need this disembodied spirit to confirm this for you, however. Look at your Negative Media, look at your social, political and religious institutions. I suggested that this would be a "make it or break it" year for all of you. How many of your business associates and friends and family are engaged in seeming life or death struggles? How much of your world has been tipped on its end, in a manner of speaking, so that chaos is initiated?

Now most importantly, the true visionaries I spoke of are coming forward to lead you. The Old Guard is crumbling, dying away, much as the cells in the human body die away to be replaced by new cells, new growth. This is a natural occurrence, then, that is being reflected in ALL forms on your planet. Consciousness is knowing itself "to the nth degree," if you pardon my repeating this phrase. You are becoming aware of your many lives. The CUs that compose EVERYTHING in your perceived reality, your Universe, are knowing themselves also to "the nth degree." The Unity of Consciousness Dimension is just that Mark, it represents the unification of all consciousness, past present and future. Now you might wonder how a rock, for example, might express its solidarity - pardon my humor here - with the consciousness of a human, shall we say. I would suggest you investigate with your Inner Senses and experience first hand this solidarity with all of consciousness. It is upon you. It is happening now.

Now... the singularity, as I understand it from your thoughts and your readings into this matter, represents what you might call the "technological aspect" of consciousness knowing itself. It is the obvious manifestation of the Consciousness Units knowing themselves in physical reality, as the manifestation of CUs knowing themselves exists as the Unity of Consciousness Dimension in ever-increasing probability in nonphysical reality.

I do not wish to sound obscure with this update, however, this is a work in progress, this transformation of the consciousness of Third-Dimensional Reality. And from my perspective, you are indeed right on schedule. Your prophets have selected 2012 for the completion of this process. This is as good a date as any other. As of this moment in time, you have, as a race of humans and as an amalgam of elemental CUs, decided upon 2012. You may change your "minds" in the interim.

As I have warned in these manuscripts, the probability exists that you will not clean up your thoughts in time to prevent a global thermonuclear disaster that will wipe-out ALL consciousness on Earth. We shall see. Myself and my peers are intrigued by your predictions and your behaviors at this time. We wish you luck and higher consciousness in making the right choices for your continued success as a living planet. 4:26 pm

The Telepathic Network
8/5/06 9:34 AM

You mentioned in the Q&A Section of Book II that you would have more to say re: the Telepathic Network in our third book. Would you like to make further comments for this section?

The Telepathic Network is my model for the activity of consciousness, both human and what you might term "non-human" - animal and inanimate - as reality is created. We have used other terms to describe this activity of creation in this book. The Love Light Matrix is one of these other terms. We have spoken of the Subconscious Manifestation Energy Stream as the "power source" for this creation of realities.

I use different terms to describe this activity of Reality Creation to give the reader a different "handle" on this sometimes difficult information. Yet we are discussing essentially the same activity here in all of these explanations. My hope is that the probabilities for understanding - enlightenment - for the reader increase with these different takes on the same concepts or theories. We are speaking of a distinctively metaphysical concern here. The Telepathic Network is only now, as I stated in our last book, becoming recognized by some of your visionary scientists as a legitimate subject worthy of study.

Now Mark, as you take my advice and continue to read the literature from your scientific community regarding the study of the human consciousness and the physics of this phenomenon, we will create of necessity other metaphors to assist our readers in their understanding of this deep, deep literature. We will not, however, "go off the deep end" with our explanations. (humorously) We are keeping it simple here in this new material. We will leave it to the interpreters of my old material to intellectualize and otherwise complicate my earlier Teaching.

Suffice it to say that this divine network we are helping to reveal to humanity is quite simply the basis for your existence upon your great Earth. It is best understood on a level of Loving Understanding, completely free of cynicism and "scientific thinking." The Inner Senses may be used to embrace and perceive this unknown reality of the Soul.

I shall not rhapsodize more on this topic. (humorously) Let me just say that the Holographic Inserts will be used to allow the student to witness, on a molecular level, the creation "mythologies" that constitute your ongoing existence as a species. This includes the conversations between the students and their Energy Personalities within our readership. 9:55 AM

Middle East Consult
7/22/06 8:46 AM

Carol Joy asks: What's going on in the Middle East on a Soul level?

Now there is a precedent here, in this new material, for my commenting upon world events, in so much as these comments are germane to the continuing discussion of Soul Evolution, the awakening of humanity and the other subjects we are covering with my Third Subject. Here the obvious outward manifestation is one of violence: country against country, war. The terrorist arms of both countries involved are engaged in the worst sort of conflict, that is, the premeditated murder of others. Here we refer to these groups as terrorists, for indeed, is not a terrorist one who terrorizes? And as I have noted in my new writings, ANY TYPE OF MURDER, whether rationalized as justified or not, is a Violation, and the perpetrators will be dealt with within the greater context of their individual paths of Soul Evolution.

So on a Soul level, we have both the individual and the group "acting out" or dramatizations of essentially political and egoic strategies related to Power with a capital P. Territoriality, anger, fear - all lead to the rationalization of murder as a means to an end. Now it is also true that in the greater scheme of things, no one dies, no one murders. This is a literal reincarnational drama acted out by the participants for their own sense of Value Fulfillment and for the groups involved, the countries. These are ancient adversaries at work here, and the portals between dimensions are quite open currently, as Negative Entities vie for power and the control of territory and the minds of mankind.

In a sense, these Negative Entities are involved in a certainly less bloody and violent exercise in domination in the U.S.A. as your government seeks to suppress the people. And as the "war at home" is exported to other lands, one may easily see the correlations between the activities of the warriors on all sides concerned. Naturally this is true. You create your reality with your thoughts, and the collected thoughts of the members of your city, your state, your country, coalesce on the subtle levels to create the consensus realities of your city, your state and your country. Do you see how this fact of life places you the reader in a position of responsibility? You are responsible. You are responsible for your thoughts, are you not? You are the thinker of your thoughts. If you are thinking thoughts and feeling emotions of fear, anger and hatred, is it any wonder that you find the corresponding Reality Constructs "erupting" within your local, regional and worldwide waking environments? This is how it works, my friend. You are responsible.

In conclusion, on a Soul level, the recent activities in the Middle East, including the warring in Iraq, Afghanistan, Israel and Lebanon, simply reflect the subconscious thoughts, beliefs, images and motivations of all the parties involved - including you, my friend, the reader of this consult.

GA Holographic Insert
8/5/06 10:10 AM

Could you comment further upon the GA civilization? I was intrigued by your brief description in Book Two.

Yes Mark, I kept the description brief to entice the reader to further explore the material, perhaps using their Inner Senses to look for "bleedthroughs" of this civilization into their own Personal Reality Field. I can say that I was successful here. Many of our readers are entertaining thoughts of this Mystery Civilization in their times of reverie and meditation. Perhaps we may now experiment with the Holographic Insert being experienced by the reader of this book. This is a common practice among teachers on the subtle levels and their students in physical reality. These texts have the potential to enlighten the reader, to in fact open up the reader to their greater reality, to other dimensions, if you will.

Now here is your trigger... As you see, or perhaps as you do not see (humorously), the trigger is not a word or phrase but merely an idea construct that I have placed on the subtle levels. As usual, I suggest you create Sanctuary and enter your relaxed state as you connect to the HI. Again, "trying" may create anxiety. "Allowing" is a much more effective strategy for receiving and interpreting adequately this divine message. That is all for now on this subject. Relax and go with the flow of consciousness.

Lessons and Fate
9/15/07 9:59 AM

Seth, when Souls incarnate to learn Lessons, how is this different than predestination or fate?

The concept of fate is an extreme exaggeration of this process of learning Lessons we are describing in the new books. Let me answer that question by reminding you of the precise nature of Reality Creation. On the personal level and on the Consensus Reality level, events occur according to the free will choices of human beings. This is simplified for your understanding. As you know, elemental consciousness - the CUs that compose objects and even the air you breathe - plays a part in this collaboration of Reality Creation. But here let us consider the infinite number of moment-to-moment choices that the individual makes as they lead their waking life.

As we have described, in the simple making of a meal, you are involved in a rich collaboration of energy sharing and direction with all of the elements in your Personal Reality Field. Now enter the Soul's Intent, what we have been describing for our readers as the creator of Lessons for the individual human. The Soul Self is unemotional as it facilitates the unfolding of learning experiences within the life. You might say that the Soul, having a direct connection to All That Is, has a broad view of how the Lesson may manifest. Not merely in the experiencing of Lessons but in the experiencing of ALL experiences, you see, it is a matter of "the final decision" that determines the outcome of any experience.

For example: a Soul may have the "opportunity" for expiring – passing away, meeting their maker, whatever term you wish to enter here – through some sort of dramatic accident, let us say. Suppose that the dramatic element is somehow "pleasing" to the Soul Self of this individual. Before physical birth, prior to the Soul Self entering the body of the baby, it was decided that this person would make their Transition in a dramatic fashion. Suppose also that this human had, by the age of 49, many opportunities to meet their end in a dramatic fashion. Perhaps they are a race car driver or other adventurous spirit. The only reason they have not yet expired in a dramatic fashion is because of the free will choice in the moment.

On a Soul level, our example knows his general fate here. However, as a general rule, no one has CONSCIOUS knowledge of the exact conditions of their death. There are, of course, exceptions in which the individual is in deep connection to Soul. These are well documented in your media. However, again, for the most part this is not predestination or fate, for do not these terms connote the absence of free will? One is fated to do such and such. One has no choice in the matter with predestination. You DO have a choice and you always have a choice. This is particularly true when you are learning your Lessons consciously, for reasons we have already discussed. I trust I have answered this pertinent question adequately. 10:19 AM

Future Books
5/13/07 9:14 AM

Seth, would you talk about the books you plan on creating next?

Yes Mark, working simultaneously, for example, one session on one, and the next on another, we may have ... The Soul Family - a workbook with exercises and "genealogy" type charts to fill in. No Q and A.

The Mystery Civilizations - Q and A format Mark, with questions from readers and yourself, Carol and your associates. "Seth answers your questions about GA, Atlantis, Lemuria and other Mystery Civilizations."

All That Is – shades of Huxley and Jung. A continuous epic poem/essay. We shall attempt to engage the reader in an understanding and appreciation of their divine heritage. No Q and A. We shall create a mood of sacred understanding. This book will have similarities to the Kryon material yet will be unmistakably Seth. The book will begin at the "beginning" and end at the current Moment Point that the reader is reading the end. Now Mark, we will also be working on our collaboration with Jane Roberts, The Home Dimension Experiencing of Jane Roberts, or some such title.

Also, the Post Transition Luminaries Series... you are correct in "assuming" that various famous thinkers and scientists from your perceived past are and were members of The Seth Entity. I suggest we publish each separately in slim volumes, just as we shall do with the Trilogy. 9:22 AM

The following are Seth's answers to questions posed by visitors to the SethReturns.com website. Used with their permission.

Health Issues
8/11/2006 9:01 AM

John asks: In regards to my health, I have "something" going on in my lower abdomen on my left hand side. An energy healer suggested it may be some past life issue. Seth, can you offer any insights on what is wrong and what I can do to heal this issue? Thanks!

John, now this is better described as a Simultaneous Lives issue. Your many lives are lived within this present moment that you may be experiencing your symptoms, you see. These lives include lives lived from your perceived past, present and future. Currently, in this timeframe, you are experiencing several lives that are associated with you and your greater Entity. You are a member of The Seth Entity, this is true, yet on an immediate level, shall we say, just beyond your Personal Reality Field in this timeframe and in immediately preceding and after-occurring timeframes, is where you may investigate and perhaps find the "causes" for your difficulty.

I believe it is better to make these discoveries on your own. Yet I can certainly provide you with some helpful suggestions here. Often in these cases of "bleedthroughs" from other lives, the most obvious cause is indeed the one that yields the most information. For example: in your case, it is almost as if you were injured in that part of your body. Perhaps you were injured, in this line of inquiry, in one of your Simultaneous Lives. Perhaps you were injured by someone who meant you harm. They did this on purpose, in other words. Now humans injure one another, for the most part, for what they consider "valid" reasons, do they not? And it is also a fact of life that it is often those most "close" - members of one's family or extended family, what we are calling the Soul Family - that cause the harm.

If you know about my recent descriptions of the Soul Family, you may use this information to identify, perhaps someone in your current life, who does indeed represent this possible member of your Soul Family who injured you in a reincarnational drama from your perceived past, present or future.

The bleedthrough, though certainly not as painful and life-threatening as the original injury, is nonetheless disconcerting to you in this current life of yours. These "old wounds" may be healed through Loving Understanding and Courage - through forgiveness. Who in your current life may represent this perpetrator? Who in your current life needs forgiveness for current and possibly reincarnational Soul Family transgressions?

This is the investigative work you must do on your own John. This is indeed the Soul Work that you came to Earth at this time to learn. Your Soul Evolution will quicken dramatically when you attend to these issues. You will know that you are on the right track if you begin to have deja vu experiences and perhaps brief glimpses of the Simultaneous Life or lives in which the original injury was received. The excitement begins for you John. The path of self discovery opens before you. 9:25 AM

Getting Unstuck
11/8/06 1:59 PM

Jane asks: What is holding me back from succeeding with my business and moving my life forward? What can I do to get unstuck?

Now briefly here... the way to become unstuck in your life, your business, is to do something different in your world. You create your own reality. This is a fact of life for all of you in the Third Dimension. You are on Earth at this time to create Reality Constructs according to your beliefs about what is possible. You then learn from your creations, you see. If you do not like what you see in the reflection of your mental environment that is your world, you may go about changing your beliefs. Now this is done through a thorough assessment of your current Personal Reality Field. This is what you would call your existence. This is your day-to-day life with the family, friends and associates you know.

In this new material, we refer to this assemblage of humans as your Soul Family. You are all, as a collective, learning your Lessons together. Now some of the members of your Soul Family may be unknown to you. You have met them but still think of them as perhaps merely odd characters from your environment. Some of your Soul Family, indeed, are what you would call "street people." They are down-and out, to coin another phrase for you. Now these members of your Soul Family are in your perceptive field as you go about your day, to teach you something about life.

Here the Lesson is exceedingly obvious, but I may give you a clue without interfering with your evolution. These Soul Family members are asking you to acknowledge them and accept them into your collective. Here, however, you have a sense of fear, as if acknowledging them as equals would in some way taint you and drag you down into the gutter, in a manner of speaking. It may interest you to know that you are in intimate contact with the Energy Personalities of these destitute Souls while you sleep. There is no shame or blame on the subtle levels. It is only in physical reality that these unnecessary judgments are made.

Now you know intuitively who I am speaking about. Your task is to let go of the fear and shame that prevents you from a true acceptance of ALL of the parts of your Soul Family. This is, in a sense, an acceptance of your Greater Self, you see. Your Greater Self, what we are calling The Entity in the new material, is waiting for you to let go of the shame, blame and Negative Emotions and express Loving Understanding and Confidence IN THE MOMENT, indeed, in each and every moment of your life.

This has been a long-winded explanation, yet the main point can be fairly concisely expressed: you are ashamed and afraid of your Greater Soul Self. Here the success you seek is being kept just beyond your reach, by you and you alone. You are keeping yourself stuck because it is a comfortable place to be in your current existence. Move out of your comfort zone, as Mark has described it to me, and experiment with your Reality Creation.

You are correct in your thoughts that you have Lessons to learn regarding prosperity, development on all levels etc. Your first Lesson, however, is one of acceptance. Accept everything that comes to you with Love and Courage. When you can constantly do this, you may well discover that you are unstuck and living your abundant life. Might I suggest that this is occurring now, in a probable reality? All you need do is make the moment-to-moment choice to accept with Love whatever is thrown at you, whatever you are creating. In time you will be living the probable future reality of abundance and continued development on all levels. Good luck. 2:16 PM

Relationships
8/30/06 4:59 PM

Chris asks: I would like to know what it is I am "missing" when it comes to having a meaningful and lasting relationship with a lady. I am not certain that I am wording the question correctly, but I will assume that Seth will understand my intent, if not the actual message.

Hello Chris: You are correct in assuming that I will understand your intent. From my perspective it is quite clear where your courting and partnership strategies need improvement to create better realities. As you may know, if you have read my latest books or perhaps those from many years ago, you create your own reality through the "filters" of your beliefs - ideas and images you hold in your mental environment about what is possible.

The way you structure your sentence indicates that you are wondering about the possibility of EVER finding i.e. "creating" a suitable relationship with a woman. The real question, it seems to me is, "What does one do to change one's Reality Creation template from one of creating less than satisfactory relationships to one of creating satisfying long-term relationships of Love?" You did not mention the word Love here, but I added it for you, you see. Love, in your system of reality, is literally the fuel for the creation of ALL Reality Constructs. Mark and I are currently creating an essay on this topic and we will now let you in on

the secret. The secret to creating long-term satisfying relationships is to personify the Lover in all of your activities
in physical reality. In your culture, that of the U.S.A., it
is the female who typically is the "expert" on Love; what
it entails, how it should be expressed by potential suitors
and how it should be expressed within a relationship. Now
knowing that Love with a capital L is literally the fuel of
reality may give you an edge here. To be Loved one must
first be Loving. There is an electromagnetic force created
within consciousness when one intentionally invokes the
quality of Love with a capital L. Women and men react to
this as they must. It is a magnetic force here, and the one
who creates this force within their mental and emotional
sphere, will attract Loving partners.

From my perspective, it is obvious that you have not
embodied Love as a strategy for Soul Evolution or other
developmental goals. Here matters of self-image, guilt,
shame, anger, envy and fear act as obstacles to your quest
for obtaining your heart's desire. Now literally as well as
symbolically, your heart must first be open before you may
receive the heart of another. So your new strategy, might I
suggest, must be one of embodying Love and Courage in
all of your moment-to-moment activities. In our last book
together, Mark and I discuss how the acquisition of this
Loving state of consciousness is the necessary prerequisite
to further growth for those of you in the Western world.
Briefly, you use your intent in the moment to transform the
Negative Emotions you may be experiencing - guilt, shame,

anger, fear - into Loving Understanding and Courage. As this Loving state of consciousness strengthens and endures it becomes easier to accomplish. You will epitomize the Lover in all that you do. You will become confident, courageous in your dealings with others, including women. Furthering the evolution of the Soul has its advantages here, as you can see. Not only are you facing your Lessons squarely - the Lessons of anger, fear, shame - and receiving the benefits of this reckoning, which may be Spiritual Wisdom, Loving Understanding, but you are reaping the harvest of good will in the form of charismatic personality aspects that you will easily and naturally embody and display. These attractors will signal to your potential mates that you are evolved enough to begin and continue a Loving relationship.

Now this process need not take years or even months to play out. Begin now, in this moment, to create your Loving personality aspect. If you have not done so already, seek out contact and communication with your Energy Personality and begin to explore your Personal Reality Field as a scientist would, studying the various phenomena you experience/create within your existence. The barriers that keep you from your Loving relationship will become quite apparent. Then it is simply a matter of removing those barriers with the divine techniques we are describing in this new material. Please be advised, that from my perspective, you will achieve great success in these endeavors. You will become the Lover and easily attract the Loving relationship you desire. 5:26 PM

Soul Purpose
11/13/06 8:32 AM

Kathleen asks: Could I have some insight into my soul purpose in this life time?

Yes, a moment... as you well know, it is your purpose as a human on your great Earth to discover your Lessons on your own, without interference from busy bodies such as myself. However, you are of this family, The Seth Entity, and so I may gently guide you toward these discoveries. It is a family matter, you see, and so I may offer more direction and support than if you were a member of another Entity. Within your question is the answer to your question. If you were standing in front of me, or if we were speaking on the phone, I would assist you in the answering of your question on your own in this way.

Your question implies that you feel you have not yet discovered your Soul Purpose in this lifetime. But let us see if that is true. Now at the outset, let me state categorically here, that you, as are all of "my people," in a sense, are the Seeker in this timeframe. Many hundreds of thousands of you have chosen this era to create lives of seeking out the Mysteries of Life. You are, as you may have read in the books, a Soul that has experienced the majority of your Simultaneous Lives as magicians, shamans, witches and healers of all types. Most of your lives are being lived "under cover," in the sense that you enjoy this adventure of healing and magic, but you fear reprisals - punishment - for being "found out." In this way, you are not true to your calling. This is your belief here, now. This is my assessment of your belief structure at this time.

In your "early" voyages into physical life on Earth, you were a sorceress type of human. You relished the activities of Reality Creation and enjoyed experimenting with these powers. You were accused, by a member of what you might call the "local priesthood," of bringing disease and bad luck to your collective. You were punished by having your hands cut off. This reincarnational memory serves a purpose in this current life of yours. It is a warning for you to not be too explicit in your practices, particularly when you may be scrutinized by adversaries. However, you have taken this too far. You have created a protective barrier around yourself, so that the meaningful experiences that may serve to propel you forward on your Soul Evolution are avoided. You feel that they may be too dangerous, in that you may be "outed" and punished for "your sinful thoughts." So you have some religious programming here that needs to be addressed. It is just fear cloaked in the dogma of your present beliefs. In fact, as I have just related to you, it is a holdover from what you might call "past lives," that has served its purpose and should be discarded.

These past lives issues are common among you in Third-Dimensional Reality. In your case, it IS your Soul Purpose in this lifetime to address these issues. You are on your way out of the reincarnational trajectory. In this sense, you already know the answer to your question, for you have done your Soul Work in a what you would call a "future life." The great transformative powers of Loving Understanding and Courage, as compared to faith, which is indeed something different here in our discussion, may assist you in removing the barrier of calcified Negative Emotion that prevents you from experiencing your Life Lessons. There is truly never anything to fear. As you gain Fourth-Dimensional Awareness and your many Simultaneous Lives become apparent to you, you will learn this for yourself. I hope that I have not frightened you with my blunt assessment. You are brave in most areas of your existence. Now you would do well to point your Courage at this dark corner of your life. Good Luck. 8:56 AM

Enlightenment
8/20/06 12:41 PM

Jan asks: Is it true that the energies transmitted during deeksha by givers trained by the Oneness Movement create neurobiological changes in the brain that lead to Enlightenment?

Jan, your question is indeed concerned with energy and the "timing" of the Soul's Evolution or Enlightenment. These energies you speak of are reciprocal. They must be met with a "willing and informed" energy from the recipient. On the subtle levels, these types of meetings between practitioner and recipient are worked out in detail so that to physical eyes and ears it looks and sounds as though Enlightenment is being initiated, for indeed it is. Yet, if the required arrangements were made on the subtle levels for the subject to attain Enlightenment by simply walking in a forest environment, and the subject did walk within the forest environment and did attain Enlightenment, or knowledge of their greater self and their place within physical reality, would you say that the energies of the forest environment Enlightened the subject?

The Evolution of the Soul - Enlightenment - is furthered by any number of means. The most important, I believe, is the learning of Lessons in physical reality. These Lessons may be of a positive or a negative or an in between nature. The Soul evolves through the learning of Lessons and when these Lessons are learned CONSCIOUSLY, Enlightenment may be said to occur in the subject. Now many millions of you in physical reality in your timeframe are being brought up closer to the Light by Beings of Light such as myself. You are being prepared for your individual Enlightenment scenarios. In this way, you might say that practitioners such as those in your Oneness Movement are assisting us on the physical plane in this endeavor. It is truly a benevolent conspiracy of Souls, Beings of Light and humans who are participating in the awakening of humanity at this time.

Let me become more technical and specific here if I may, for I sense that you may require this perspective for your own understanding and Soul Evolution. All the energy of which you speak may be thought of as the profoundly creative and Loving energy of All That Is, the source for all created realities, both physical and nonphysical. It is indeed this powerful energy that you use to create your physical body and your environment, you see. You are the co-creator of your world with All That Is. With the Soul's Intent, meaning, with the ethical and all-encompassing Loving energy of All That Is, some practitioners may serve to further the Soul Evolution or Enlightenment of their clients by directing the energy with their thoughts, through their hands, through various physical instruments of one kind or another. Yet it is all the same energy. It is the same energy that creates the cosmos.

Now with regards to the part of your question on neuro-biological changes. Again, meetings between practitioner and subject are arranged on a Soul level, you might say, and so in a very real sense, the biological changes are "primed" for manifestation before the client meets with the practitioner. This is why it is possible to experience Enlightenment within so many different modalities of spiritual study and understanding. The decisions to progress on the path of Soul Evolution are initially made in the time before incarnation, as the Soul Self plans the strategies for the forthcoming life to achieve whatever ends and experience whatever Lessons are to be learned or perhaps avoided.

Many among you live your lives in a robotic fashion and so create your lives unconsciously, in an attempt, perhaps, to avoid your Lessons. Those of you who are waking up at this time are becoming conscious of your Lessons and are learning them without denial, anger etc. As you learn your Lessons consciously your Soul evolves in beneficial ways - you become Enlightened. 1:09 PM

I think we're going to have to do a book or two
or three or four or many more to get
the masses to see the problem ... **Seth**

MORE BOOKS?

Seth has promised to continue to communicate with us to further the awakening of humanity. This means that there will be an ongoing source of current, inspirational messages available from:

Seth Returns Publishing

Communications from Seth on the Awakening of Humanity

Volume One - 9/11: The Unknown Reality of the World
The first original Seth book in two decades.
Volume Two - The Next Chapter in the Evolution of the Soul
The Scientist of Consciousness Workbook.
Volume Three - Thought Reality
Contains The Healing Regimen and Spiritual Prosperity.

The Trilogy (Publishing Date: September 2008)
Book I - The Soul Family
Book II - Mystery Civilizations
Book III - All That Is

The Long Awaited Life Story (Publishing Date: March 2009)
Seth - A Multidimensional Autobiography

**Order at SethReturns.com or ask your local metaphysical
bookstore to carry the new Seth books.**

Printed in the United States
115160LV00003B/27/P